THE
LAST
CHAPTER

THE
LAST
CHAPTER

by A. W. Rasmussen

Whitaker House

Whitaker House
504 Laurel Drive
Monroeville, Pennsylvania 15146

© 1973 by Whitaker House

Printed in the United States of America

ISBN 0-88368-021-1

Printings
First Edition 1973—25,000 Copies
Second Edition 1974—25,000 Copies

CONTENTS

Preface

My father, the Reverend A. W. Rasmussen, D.D., is a Spirit-filled minister of the Gospel and overseer of the Independent Assemblies of God International which he incorporated in 1964. He has served as pastor of churches from the Atlantic to the Pacific. He is the founder of Chicago Bible College in Chicago, Illinois, and Temple Bible College in Edmonton, Alberta, Canada. He is also the director of Mantle Missions which has a worldwide outreach in training the national ministry of various countries, supporting nationals, helping to support orphans, building native churches and supporting Gospel radio broadcasts.

I have great respect and a deep love for this man, my father, who does not claim to have

9

attained but is forever striving forward for the prize of the high calling of God in Christ Jesus.

The Last Chapter is a most optimistic message about the last days of the Church and the second coming of Christ. There is also much fresh teaching here about the significance of the charismatic outpouring.

Every effort has been made to tell each episode of the story exactly as it happened. However, in order to safeguard the confidence of certain people in the story, and in order to prevent misunderstandings or embarrassment, a number of fictitious names have been used.

It is with great pleasure that I introduce my father's book to you. These pages were written for the purpose of revealing the many-sided grandeur of our Lord Jesus Christ. May your faith be strengthened in the reading of this thrilling story.

Philip A. Rasmussen
Marriage, family and child counselor

CHAPTER ONE

Anything But A Preacher!

What a Christmas Eve it was! The bitter cold wind howled and shrieked around the corners of our Minnesota farm house, and whistled through the barren poplar and box elder trees. The savage blizzard seemed to come from all directions at once, piling up into high drifts which made the barn and farm sheds practically invisible. The temperature registered at 25 below zero.

Inside the house it was warm and cozy. It was 1905; the kerosene lamps cast a mellow glow throughout the kitchen. The sweet aroma of good food filled the house. Mother Rasmussen had worked all day preparing the traditional Scandinavian Christmas Eve supper of *lute-fisk* (codfish), boiled potatoes with white sauce, and sweet fruit soup made of

11

dried raisins, apples, prunes and tapioca. She appeared a little tired as she finally sat down at the table with her husband and two spirited boys: Albin, age 5, and Arthur, age 3. Both she and her husband knew that the time was near when she would be giving birth to another child.

"When are we going to open our presents?" Albin wanted to know, as Mother loaded up his plate.

"Just as soon as supper and devotions are over, Son," Dad answered.

"Oh boy! I'm going to eat fast!" Albin exclaimed.

"Me, too!" chimed in little Arthur.

The living room was decorated with paper streamers and Christmas bells. Standing in the corner was the Christmas tree decorated with home-made ornaments and paraffin candles of red, green and white. After supper the family gathered around the tree and prayed. Dad asked the boys to recite their Christmas pieces which they would give at the church Christmas program on December twenty-sixth. After that, the boys tore the wrappings off their gifts with gleeful laughter.

About ten o'clock that night, after the boys had gone to bed, Mother Rasmussen said to her husband, "Honey, I think the time has come. You'd better call Dr. Johnson."

"Are you sure?" he asked.

"Yes."

Quickly he went to the old telephone and made the call. "Doc," he said hesitatingly, "I hate to call you out on a night like this, but my wife is going to have the baby. You'd better come right away."

The doctor lived in Willmar, about seven miles from the farm. Both Dad and Mother Rasmussen breathed a prayer that he would be able to make it. Even the mailman hadn't been able to get through for days due to the heavy drifting. But good old Doc! With his horse and sleigh, he fought his way through the snowstorm, and arrived around 11 o'clock. At 11:30 I was born.

"Cute one, ain't he?" Dad said.

"Yes," Mother observed drily, "but he might at least have waited until after dinner tomorrow!"

"Well, Mother," Dad said, "don't you worry about little details like that. We'll take care of everything."

"And who is 'we?' " she asked, with a mischievous twinkle in her eye.

"Well, er—," he stammered, "you know how Aunt Hannah always enjoys helping at a time like this."

"Yes," Mother replied, teasing, "and we *do* want Hannah to have her share of joy, don't we?"

Dad acted like he didn't hear her, and just stood there beaming over his new baby boy.

Dad was a God-fearing Dane who never missed a service in our rural Lutheran Church near Pennock, Minnesota. Almost everyone around Pennock knew Dad well and respected his desires to have a Christian family. Mother was a stalwart Swede whose presence blessed our home with more than enough sunshine. I look back to those happy days with gratitude, remembering clearly the holy atmosphere of our home, and the love which flowed so freely.

I started thinking on the big subject of God one summer at the age of 5. Tumbling around in the grass in front of our farmhouse was lots of fun. Everything was new then. The breeze running its slithery fingers through my hair was new. The sweet smell of the grass was new. The warmth of the sunshine made me run and skip and giggle.

As I lay there in the soft grass, I looked up into the immense blue dome above me and watched the white clouds lazily drifting by. It was fun, just lying there "thinkin'." Dad had often told us about God up in Heaven, and it seemed like the most natural thing in the world to wonder about Him, and if He was really up there beyond the clouds.

"There *must* be a God up there—'cause if there isn't, then who made the sky—and who made the grass? (I wish I had a jelly sandwich.)"

I crossed my little legs and folded my

chubby hands under my head. A butterfly flittered by.

"God must've made the stars too—and the moon—and the summer—and winter . . . ."

Then an extraordinary thing happened. I felt as though the great God of the heavens came down over me; I was surrounded by His presence—so much so that all I could do was just lie there very still. Then He spoke to me. How, I cannot tell you. But there came to me the clearest impression of these words:

"Be faithful—and always walk humbly before Me—and the day will come when I will use you."

The impression left on my heart was so deep that it never left.

Even in my school years, the idea followed me. I had to walk about a mile and three-quarters to and from school. As I tramped through the fields and meadows, there were times when that same divine Presence I had felt on our front lawn would envelop me again. In my imagination (or was it in visions?) I would see myself standing before vast congregations, preaching the Gospel with unusual power. My spirit burned within me as I thundered out the message.

I am convinced now that these were more

15

than childish daydreams. I believe this was God's way of showing me the direction my life was to take. He was telling me that I would have at least a small role to play in *something great* He was about to do. Little did I know what that *something* was: *that God was getting ready to wrap up the last great chapter in the earthly history of the Church before the return of Christ; that the Holy Spirit would be poured out upon the Church with spectacular signs and wonders; that hundreds and thousands of people from every corner of the globe would be swept into the kingdom of God.* I understood none of those things then.

By the time I was approaching my teens, however, I secretly hoped that God would change His mind and let me be something else: maybe a fireman or a great explorer—*anything* but a preacher! But no matter how hard I tried to get Him to change, the same thought about the ministry kept making a nuisance of itself.

"Hey, Dad!" I finally blurted out one day. "What would you say if I became a preacher when I grow up?"

His eyes began to glisten with tears. "Andrew," he said solemnly, "I have always prayed to God that one of my sons would enter the ministry. In fact, before you were born, I dedicated you to God for that very purpose."

Before I was born! I thought and thought about those words. Could it be that God had His hand upon me in some unusual way even before my birth?

I remembered that Dad had read to us from the Bible about God's sanctifying Jeremiah before he was born. And wasn't the same thing true of John the Baptist? I was pretty sure I could find that passage without too much trouble, so I leafed through my Bible until I found it. There it was in Luke 1:15:

"He shall be filled with the Holy Ghost,
even from his mother's womb."

"Wow!" I thought. "God actually *does* call people before they're born!"

Noticing another reference printed in the center column of my Bible, I quickly turned over to Galatians 1:15. There I read that God separated Paul from his mother's womb, and call him by His grace.

I pondered over those verses for some time. It seemed very clear that God sometimes calls His servants even while they are yet unborn. It was an almost mysterious thought—as though there were some kind of prenatal anointing for us which only God could determine.

"Lord," I asked, "what have you got in store for me?" But He would tell me nothing more at that time. The story remained to be written, chapter by chapter.

All eight of us worked hard on the farm. We always got up around 5 in the morning and went out to the barn with Dad to help milk the cows and get the other chores done. Then around 6:30 or 7:00, we'd head for the house, hungry as bears. As soon as we opened the back door, what a tantalizing aroma would meet our noses! The breakfasts Mother cooked were out of this world. Not little sissy breakfasts—but big, he-man meals that would stick to our ribs. After grace, everybody would get a big scoop of steaming hot *finker*, a mouth-watering pork-and-apple treat which Mother always made when we butchered. Then there were lots of home-fried potatoes, slabs of fried pork, tall pitchers of milk and stacks of home-made rye bread.

By 7:30, we'd be out in the fields, and we'd work hard until sundown. Of course, Mother always had a king-size dinner for us at noon. That was the main meal of the day, and a time of laughter and relaxation. Soon, though, we'd be back out in the fields, stopping only briefly to wolf down the lunches Mother sent out to tide us over until supper.

We never went anywhere. But there was a kind of sweet security about the quietness of the farm life and our Christian home which proved to be a great factor in the way my life turned out. Since those days, I've often pondered the tremendous impact of parents on children. I doubt if mothers and fathers know how deep an impression they make on their children. It's an awesome thought. What greater heritage can any child have than Christian parents who know God and are led by His Spirit?

The Holy Spirit began working on me in an intensified way when I was 13. An evangelist by the name of A. B. Ost came to the village to hold a revival. The services were held in the evenings over at the old Pennock school- house. Our family was there every night; but one night in particular stands out in my mind.

I always enjoyed the singing; one song we sang that night was *"Brighten the Corner Where You Are."* How we sang it! The rafters in that old school building fairly vibrated with the joyful noise. After a simple Gospel message, the moment of invitation came. "How many here will accept Jesus as their Savior?" the evangelist wanted to know. As I sat there listening and watching, great convic- tion took hold of me. I trembled within as I realized for the first time that *I* needed a Sav- ior.

There is nothing quite so hard for the world to understand as this. Why should an already *religious* person need salvation? Especially one so young.

"He's only a child," we protest.

"And he's such a *good* boy!"

"He never misses church!"

"Saved? Saved from *what?*"

"Isn't this rather ridiculous?"

So we reason. That's why I'm convinced that there isn't a miracle much greater than that which takes place when the Holy Spirit reveals the need of salvation to an already "good" person. We all want to retreat into our self-righteousness, and declare ourselves good enough. But that night I saw that all of my supposed goodness was only as "filthy rags" in the sight of God, and I saw that I needed Jesus.

The evangelist was pressing his invitation home to the waiting congregation with great power. As he left the pulpit and worked his way out through the people, inquiring of various ones about their need of Jesus, I knew that my moment had come. The decision had to be made. In a few moments, a number of other zealous soul-winners in the congregation were milling around, noticing people who seemed to be under conviction, and urging them to receive Jesus. Finally, one of them stood beside me.

"Andrew, would you like to accept Jesus as your Savior?"

Swallowing my pride in one big gulp, I answered, "Yes."

I meant it from the depths of my heart.

20

And it turned out to be the biggest "Yes" of my life.

Many changes followed, especially in the deeper recesses of my own spirit. My life became centered in Jesus in a new way. I knew now that my life was not my own; it belonged to Him.

Yet in many ways I was not different from other boys my age. The problem of submitting to discipline was an especially big pain. I will never forget that hot summer day when I was out in the front yard studying my catechism. I was leaning against the old doghouse, going over and over the answers to every question, while hunchback bees buzzed in the dandelions. My younger sisters, Myrtle and Eleanor, were in the house helping Mother with her work and looking after baby Richard. My other brothers, Al, Art and Eddie were up at the barn with Dad.

"Andrew!" I heard my Dad call. "Come on up here!"

Since I had just gotten started on my catechism, I pretended I didn't hear him.

"Aaaandrooooo!" he bellowed. "Come on, we've got work to do!" He was coming closer now.

"Uh-oh," I thought, "maybe I'd better answer him."

In a moment I could feel his penetrating gaze on the back of my neck. "Andrew, I'm *calling* you."

"I— I'm sorry, Dad," I stammered, turning to see him standing there with both hands on his hips. "I heard you call, but I've just *got* to get this catechism memorized, and I thought . . . ." (What I really thought was that my catechism was more important than his old farm work. After all, the catechism was *religious* stuff!)

"Andrew," he said quietly but firmly, "I need you *right now*. I want you to come up to the barn and help us get the binder ready for harvesting."

"Ahhh, Dad . . . ."

"No 'Ah-Dads'," he insisted. "I'm glad you're interested in the catechism, but you'll have time for that later. Right now the harvest is ripe, and we must get out into the fields."

With a sigh, I put the catechism down and went off to the barn, grumbling to myself all the way. Many years passed before I understood that obeying my father was indeed obeying the Word of God.

CHAPTER TWO

"Follow the Tall Man!"

When I was sixteen, I left home to go find a job and save up some money for my education. I had no desire to grow up and be a farmer, and there were three brothers and two sisters who could help my father and mother with the work.

I went to the big city of Minneapolis—the promised land of job opportunities. But every man who interviewed me asked the same question: "What experience have you had?" When I mentioned the farm, they'd snort and make some sort of degrading remark. So I finally ended up in a labor gang with the Great Northern Railway.

If I needed anymore humbling, my first job was the right one to give it to me. I was assigned to the stockyards where they brought in cattle cars. Let it be sufficient to say that what I found on the floors of those cars wasn't Johnson's Wax. When I wrote home, I told Dad I was cleaning out *railroad* cars. I hoped he would think I meant *passenger* cars.

It was a rough life for a 16-year-old. The work was hard, the hours were long, and I was constantly subjected to the foul language and dirty jokes of the men. But the Holy Spirit still had a strong grip on my life. The more of their profanity and vulgarity I heard, the more I determined to shun it.

About a month later, my brother Al joined me, and we moved up to northern Minnesota to work in the iron mines. We made good money, and I saved up quite a substantial amount. It was a good feeling to be "successful"—and I decided to go after more of it. Forgetting all about those early visions of preaching the Gospel, I enrolled in the F. W. Dobe correspondence course in engineering. It made me feel good that I didn't have to burden my father. I was able to pay my own tuition and all other expenses. Deeply fascinated by my studies, I often caught myself daydreaming about the great success I was going to be. I was applying myself and making excellent grades—and in 2 years, I completed the course and moved to Chicago to look for a job suited to my new abilities.

It didn't take me long. I was hired by the A.B.T. Manufacturing Company, and began advancing immediately. The future looked bright for me from a material point of view. I liked the taste of success, and tried not to think about my call to the ministry. But God is faithful, and one night He spoke to me in a vision.

I saw myself standing out in a field at night. I had seen such fields many times in Minnesota. After the harvest, the farmers would plow, and the soil would be jet black. You couldn't see a straw or blade of vegetation of any kind—only that rich, black soil for miles and miles. It was that kind of field in which I was standing. Above me, the night sky was cheerless and oppressive. No moon was in the sky, nor stars.

As I stood there in that heavy darkness, I was startled to hear the voices of many people crying as though in great agony. The sound became louder; they screamed as though their pains were unbearable. I began to shudder, and wondered what this was I was hearing. Then I looked and saw Someone coming toward me out of the darkness. His face radiated an unearthly brightness.

"Jesus!" I cried, immediately recognizing my Lord. "What is this crying of anguish that I hear?"

"Come," He said, "I will show you."

He led me through the darkness for a short distance, and then we stopped. I was completely unprepared for what I was to see next.

Before us was a vast, open pit, full of fire.

"What is this?" I asked in wonderment.

"This is the bottomless pit," He said. "Look down into it."

I peered cautiously over the pit's edge. As I looked, I could see flames and fire leaping into the air. I could see thousands of men and women, young and old. They were in deep agony and distress; they were beating themselves; they were pulling their hair; they were screaming; they were beside themselves in pain. The flames would come over them in waves, the suffering rising with the waves, then subsiding again, only to rise again with the next wave of flames. I saw their flesh literally crawling with worms and maggots, just as the Bible says*, and I cringed and turned my face away from the sight. It weakened me so badly I was afraid I would fall in.

"Oh, Jesus! Save me! Save me, Jesus!" I cried.

I can still remember how He reached down to me and, putting His hands under my arms, pulled me away from the edge of the pit to more solid ground. As I stood there, still trembling, I looked toward the east and saw another strange sight.

It was in dramatic contrast to what I had just seen. The eastern sky was lit up. But the blazing light out there on the horizon was not

*Mark 9:43-48

the sun. It was different from the sun. I could look directly at it and it didn't hurt my eyes at all.

"Jesus," I asked, "what is this that I see?"

"That," He said with a smile, "is the Heavenly City, the New Jerusalem, with gates of pearl."

I stood there drinking in its beauty. It seemed all the more beautiful in contrast to what I had just seen a few moments before. A yearning for that place filled my soul.

"Oh, Jesus," I said with tear-filled eyes, "that is where I want to go." And looking back to the pit with a shudder, I added, "I never want to go there."

"My son," He said, "you may go to the Heavenly City—but only if you follow Him." And He pointed to a very tall Person who was walking by. I had not noticed Him before. He must have been around nine feet tall, and when He walked, He took very long steps.

"Am I to follow Him?" I asked myself silently. "How can I put my feet into His footprints? His legs are so much longer than mine!"

Jesus had said to follow Him though, and I knew I must start immediately or be left behind. I had to throw my body forward with all the strength I had in order to reach each succeeding step. I thought it would be very difficult, but there seemed to be an unseen

27

Presence that helped me; I found it surprisingly easy.

As I walked on and on, I noticed that the fields which had been so black and barren were now lit up with a heavenly radiance, and out of the soil that was so black there came a velvet carpet of green. This luxurious grass was growing everywhere. A bubbling stream was flowing through the fields, having its source from a towering mountain in the distance. The birds were busy waking up the morning, and the trees were blooming and filling the air with the exhilarating fragrance of spring. It was a beautiful sight!

But who was this Man who was leading the way without a word? Was it the Holy Spirit? (I knew it wasn't Jesus, since I had just talked with Him a few minutes before.) On and on we walked, getting nearer and nearer the luminous City. Just before we reached it, the vision disappeared.

The next day, the vision began to bring results. My roommate, Leonard Berry (a student at Moody Bible Institute), was getting ready to go out.

"Where are you going?" I asked.

"I'm going down to a little Gospel mission," he answered. "Want to come along?"

"I'd *love* to!" I replied, jumping at the

chance to be in a service. After what had happened the night before, I felt that I needed to be in church.

It didn't take us long to get there. Turning down Halsted Street, I saw a sign a short distance ahead: THE LIGHT OF THE WORLD MISSION.

It was just a simple Gospel meeting house for down-and-outers, but it was a good place for me to be. As I sat there listening to the student preacher, I was hardly aware of what he was saying. All I could think about was the vision I had had the night before. I knew that God was speaking to me again, to remind me of my calling to His work. It was no longer a matter of cheap options; I had to make up my mind. God was not going to force me to follow that Big Man. The choice was mine to make. I knew there could be only one answer: my engineering plans had to go.

When the young preacher extended his closing invitation, I was the first one to walk to the front of that little mission. What took place there, only God and I knew.

After it was all over, I stood and said to the people, "I'm glad that I can give my life completely and wholly to the Lord Jesus Christ."

That was a big mouthful!

I went on to say, "I'll go wherever He wants me to go. If He wants me to go to Africa to give my life for the Africans—even to die there—I'm willing to go. And if He calls me anywhere else, I'm willing to go."

Little did I know what I was saying.

I'll never forget the day, several years after my experience in the mission, when God began to talk to me about some money I owed to a man by the name of Nord. The indebtedness came about when Al and I had been working in the iron mine in northern Minnesota. We had arranged to live in a company boarding house, and the problem started the day we registered. The proprietor, Mr. Nord, forgot to put our names on his list, and we didn't bother to remind him either. When our first payday rolled around we realized immediate benefits: there were no deductions for room and board. (How lucky can you get?)

Feeling a little guilty about it, I said to Al, "Don't you think we ought to tell him?"

"Nooo," he replied, with a prankish gleam in his eye, "that's not our mistake, that's his!" And he seemed satisfied to leave it that way.

Rather than disagree with him, I chose to keep quiet about it. Every now and then I had the urge to go down and tell poor old Mr. Nord about his mistake. But Al wouldn't appreciate that. So I tried to forget about it.

Now, several years after I had quit that

job, the thing still haunted me. The unpaid figure had soared to several hundreds of dollars. I knew I couldn't put it off much longer; the check would have to be written.

First of all, I wrote a letter to see if the old fellow was still living. A few days later, I received a reply from Mrs. Nord. Her husband had been dead for three years, and she was destitute.

Immediately, I sat down at my desk and hastily scribbled out a check for $390.00. Along with the check, I enclosed a brief note of explanation:

Dear Mrs. Nord,

I was sorry to learn about the death of your good husband. Please accept my sincere and heartfelt sympathy.

Several years ago, my brother and I lived in your husband's boarding house. Unknown to him, we never paid a cent of rent during that time. So I am enclosing a check in the amount of $390. Three hundred dollars, the amount of the account for room and board, plus 6% interest for five years—a total of $90—making a grand total of $390.

God has been speaking to me to make restitution wherever possible, and this is one place where I can do so. It's wonderful to be a Christian. Do you know

Jesus? He loves you and wants to help you.

Sincerely Yours,
Andrew Rasmussen

A few days later, I received a beautiful letter from Mrs. Nord telling me how grateful she was. I was glad I had obeyed that "still small Voice" within me. I had no idea then what excitement lay ahead of me in following the Holy Spirit, but already I was learning the importance of being sensitive to "the Tall Man" in small things.

CHAPTER THREE

Now or Never

In the days that followed, God put me through a crash course in Christian growth.

I learned the basic things at the great Humbolt Park Gospel Tabernacle in Chicago, where Rev. J. O. Wester was pastor. What a privilege it was to sit under the ministry of that man of God! Great evangelists and teachers like F. F. Bosworth and Paul Rader came to explain the fundamentals of the Gospel, and I drank in every word. Gradually, my mind was opening up to truths I had never understood before. When I heard something new, I would search the Bible to see whether it was so.

It wasn't long until I began to discover the Bible teaching about water baptism. The thing that disturbed me was that all New

Testament believers were baptized in water *after* they believed, not before. I had been baptized as an infant, but I was too young to know anything about sin and repentance.

I decided to do it all over again. It would have meaning for me now that I really knew Jesus. Besides, hadn't Jesus *commanded* His followers to be baptized? And even Jesus Himself was baptized. If He needed it, then who was I not to follow His example? So I walked down into our church baptismal pool, and the pastor plunged me under the water; I came up sopping wet and sputtering, but happy that I could declare my faith in Jesus in this way.

"We think you ought to become an active member of our church," the pastor said to me one day.

"That's right," the elders added. "We need young men like you."

I thanked them for their invitation, and in a few weeks I was indeed an active member. I participated in the youth work, taught a Sunday school class, organized street meetings, held jail services and visited in hospitals.

We had a great crowd of young people, and a wonderful choir and orchestra. Not wanting to be idle for a minute, I bought a saxophone and joined the orchestra. I was there to do anything that needed to be done. I made a lot of mistakes, but the Holy Spirit was training me, and I will always thank God for the many opportunities of service that I found in that great church. I loved the pastor and his wife for what they were in God. I loved the members of that church. I was far from being perfect, but I was glad to be serving the Lord to the best of my ability.

One Saturday night when the pastor and one of the elders were away for a conference, we young people decided to have a prayer meeting over at the church. The girls decided to meet in the downstairs prayer room, while the boys would meet in the pastor's large study up on the second floor. That was the night that God decided to remind me of His anointing on my life.

We were praying in the usual fashion, when suddenly I became aware of the peculiar presence of God in that study. My prayer became stronger, and I was conscious of a great anointing of the Holy Spirit. I completely forgot about the other boys in that room. I was caught up in the Lord's presence. I prayed on and on—thirty minutes—forty-five —an hour. I couldn't stop. I was in rapture, and I hoped it would never end. When I finally came back down to earth, the rest of the boys knew that it had been something extraordinary.

"Hey, Andrew!" they exclaimed, "do you know what you were doing? You prayed a prayer five miles long!"

We talked about it until quite late that

night, and when we went home, we all knew we had been on holy ground. When the pastor came home, he surprised us all by saying something odd.

"You know," he said, "when we were in Toronto, we had the strangest impression that something unusual was taking place in the church here . . . ."

We told him all about the experience we had had in the prayer room on Saturday night. He listened intently. Finally, he turned to me and said, "Andrew, do you know what has happened to you?"

"No, sir, I don't think so," I said.

He looked at me intently. "*You* have received the baptism of the Holy Spirit!"

I had heard my pastor mention this subject before, but I didn't know much about it at that point. I knew there were some funny people called *Pentecostals* who believe that you must speak in tongues in order to receive this baptism. But I knew that *my* pastor certainly didn't believe in *that!* Whatever this experience was, though, my pastor said I had received it, and I believed him. I trusted my pastor, and if he said it, it must be true. I was happy in my new experience, and soon noticed wonderful spiritual growth taking place in my life. But I kept it to myself, and hardly told anyone except Stella.

Stella was a girl I had met back in Minnesota, when I was working as a farmhand on her Uncle Alvig's farm. She was the "hired girl." Every day she would hurry out to the fields where I was cultivating corn, and bring me my lunch. There was something about her long blond hair blowing in the breeze, and her happy blue eyes that I liked. And what a chatterbox! She always seemed excited about something, and talked on and on about everything imaginable.

Then she'd say, "Andrew, why don't you say something?" I guess I must have seemed awfully quiet in comparison to her. But our friendship grew along with the corn, and finally blossomed into love. But then she moved to Chicago to find a better job. I guess it was because of her that I too finally came to Chicago.

When I found her there in the city, she seemed even more beautiful than before. The reason, I soon discovered, was that she was now born again. From that point on, our friendship took on a completely new dimension. We attended the Humbolt Park Gospel Tabernacle together, and anything else that would bring us closer to the Lord: street meetings, jail services, hospital meetings. Many times, we just sat and talked and shared our problems and our ideas about what we wanted to do with our lives.

I have always believed that God planned our marriage. Stella had a keen sense of responsibility to the Lord, and felt the call of God to His work, just as I did. We were both excited about getting married, but the more we talked it over, the more we saw the importance of not rushing ahead of God. I will never forget the night we finally made up our minds to enroll as theological students at the Christian and Missionary Alliance Bible College in Nyack, New York.

"Stella," I said, as we strolled down the street on our way to a street meeting, "I think we ought to go to a Bible school."

"Isn't that odd?" she exclaimed. "I've been thinking about the same thing. If we're going to do anything for God, we'll just *have* to get some training somewhere."

"Where do you suggest?"

"What about the Christian and Missionary Alliance Bible College at Nyack?"

Stella's brother Leonard was a student at Nyack, and he had written to her about what a grand school it was.

"It sounds good to me," I said. "Why don't we apply for enrollment?"

"Oh, Andrew!" she said. "Do you *really* mean it?"

"Sure!"

We walked along in silence for a moment or two. I could tell she was thinking about something that was going to be hard to say.

38

"Andrew," she said finally, "you know I love you—but . . . ."

"Yes?"

"Well—don't you think it would be best if we'd wait until after graduation to get married?"

I knew it was a good suggestion. In fact, God had been talking to me along those very same lines. Of course, in the natural, we wanted to get married sooner than that. But I knew that we both needed some time alone with God and His Word. Bible school would be the perfect place.

"Okay," I said, squeezing her hand, "God's will is more important than ours."

She looked at me with tear-filled eyes that told a long story of devotion.

We received our applications ten days later. After we had filled them out, we rushed off eagerly to the pastor's office for his recommendation and signature. We felt sure he would be just as happy about the whole thing as we were. But what a surprise was awaiting us!

"Andrew," he said, taking a long breath, "you've had some wonderful experiences, and we rejoice with you . . . ."

"Yes, sir."

"But," he continued, with emphasis, "just

39

because God has blessed you doesn't necessarily mean that you should go to Bible school."

"Not go to Bible school?" I thought. "Why, I *must* go!" Stella and I exchanged puzzled glances. I had even written to my father and told him all about it, and he had been delighted that I was planning to study for the ministry. Of course, he preferred that I go to the Lutheran College and study to be a Lutheran pastor. He had even offered to send me to the University and pay all of the costs. But he knew it was my decision to make, and he rejoiced in what I had decided.

"Well, Pastor," I said, somewhat shaken by his unexpected reaction, "We feel God's call, and we think we ought to prepare ourselves for the ministry."

"I think I know how you both feel," he answered, "but, Andrew, I would not advise any young man to go into the ministry and become a preacher unless there is no other way out."

Both Stella and I were stunned. Those strange words fell over us like a cold blanket.

"Why would he say a thing like that?" we wondered. We did not understand until a good many years later that the ministry is no picnic. It remained for us to learn of the many heartaches, the heavy burdens and the misunderstandings of people.

Had we known it then, we would have understood that our pastor was not trying to stop us from doing God's will, but rather was testing the reality of our calling. If our calling was genuine, nothing could stop us. But if it were *not* genuine, then it was best that we find it out immediately.

Finally, seeing how persistent we were, he made an unexpected proposal.

"Andrew," he said, "I need help. Why don't you stay here in the church, and I'll tutor you. I'll teach you from the Word. You can help me make the calls in homes and hospitals. You can stay right here, learning and having a ministry at the same time." He raced on: "You and Stella can continue to teach the young people and hold street meetings. You can continue with your services at the mission and the hospital. I'll even give you the opportunity of preaching to our congregation occasionally!"

I could hardly believe my ears. He had said it all so quickly that I felt like asking him to repeat it. But no; it was clear enough. And he stood there silently, awaiting my reply.

It was exactly what I really wanted. Four years of school would only mean four years of waiting to get started. But here was an opportunity to start *now*.

"What an opportunity!" I thought. "To be taught in the Scriptures by such a man of God and, at the same time, to receive valuable practical experience!" I could desire nothing better.

41

Stella and I never sent our applications to Nyack. The pastor kept every promise to us, and we were soon happily involved in the busy life of the church, although it was necessary for me to continue working for the A.B.T. Manufacturing Company in order to make ends meet.

After a few weeks of sheer delight in my new responsibilities at the church, Stella and I decided there was no more point in waiting to get married. So we made the necessary arrangements, and on September 4, 1926, the pastor married us. That night we boarded a lake steamer and started across Lake Michigan for a short honeymoon trip.

For a while after getting back to Chicago, we felt sure that great things were in store for us. I was happy in my work, and had a clear sense of divine guidance about what I was doing. It seemed to be an ideal arrangement.

I often thought of the many young men who would have given anything to be in my position. With a ministry in a good church, a lovely Christian wife, a privately tutored education and a good job as Assistant Superintendent at A.B.T. Manufacturing Company, what more could I desire? Soon we would be able to launch out into the Lord's work full time. But all too soon, something went wrong.

Elder Bill Lassen announced to the church one Sunday that the pastor was critically ill in Florida, where he had gone for rest and meditation. For some time, he had been feeling the need of getting away for a rest, and all of us had hoped that this little vacation would do him good. So it came as quite a shock to us when we heard of his illness, and we began praying earnestly for his recovery.

None of us realized how sick he was. I kept hoping he'd soon get better so I could get on with my studies. But it never happened. Within a short time, he went home to be with the Lord.

Immediately, I was plunged into all kinds of confusion. Nothing made any sense. With that man went all my hopes of an education and all my opportunities for the ministry. All was swept away in one cruel stroke. I knew the church would be looking for a new pastor. Suddenly, I was back where I started.

"What are we going to do?" I asked Stella, in despair. We talked it over, and Stella chattered on and on about different possibilities, and tried to cheer me up with her Norwegian sense of humor.

But she knew as well as I did we were backed into some kind of corner. There seemed to be only one thing to do. I would have to forget about the ministry and plan for a career in engineering. It made me heartsick to think of it, but I thought I had no other choice. I felt guilty about the whole thing, for I remembered so clearly how God had previously dealt with me about His will for my life. I had not yet learned that God often has many surprises for us, and that all He wants us to do is trust Him for the outcome.

When I again began to put my full attention to my job at A.B.T. Manufacturing, the old comfortable feeling gradually came back. I really enjoyed supervising the men, and now that I wasn't spending so much time in Bible study, there was lots more time for self-improvement. So I began to study all I could on the side in order to develop my skills even more extensively.

"It's not so bad," I reasoned with Stella. "I'm in a good profession, and I'm making a lot more money than I ever could in the ministry. I'll have lots money to give to the church and missions."

"Andrew Rasmussen," she said with a twinkle in her eye, "where's your faith? If God wants you in the ministry, won't He make a way?"

I grinned at her sheepishly. "Sure, I guess He will—but look at it this way. I'll probably be doing more good by giving all this money than by being in the ministry. And besides, I can still help out down at the church with different odds and ends."

"Andrew," she said, "you're rationalizing!"

44

And she planted a kiss on my cheek and walked out into the living room.

"Hmph," I said to myself, "I do believe the lady is right!" But at the moment, I couldn't see any other alternative than going on with my job.

As the months rolled by, I actually began to believe that God was guiding me—especially when the opportunity to work at Fisher X-ray turned up. They were offering me an even better position than I had at A.B.T. Finally, after some careful consideration, I resigned my supervisory job and was hired by Fisher as a mechanical engineer in design.

The boss liked my work, and soon the results began showing up on my paycheck. Even Stella was proud of me. I was feeling pretty good about the whole matter, until the day I decided to work over the lunch hour.

I had been given a big assignment to design a new piece of equipment. It was an important job for us, and I wanted to give it my best. The noon hour was a good time to concentrate, because everyone else had gone out for lunch. Besides, I had decided to fast all of my noon meals and give my lunch money to missions.

The office was as quiet as an old attic, the only sound being the scratching of my pencil and the occasional rattle of paper. Working at a drawing board demanded a great deal of concentration. I was deeply absorbed in my project when I heard someone speak.

"*Now or never*," the voice said.

I whirled around quickly to see who the intruder was. But there was no one. The door was shut, and the office was completely empty. There was no one but me.

"That's odd," I said to myself. "Must've been my imagination . . . ." I pondered the matter for a fleeting moment, then busied myself with my work.

I was just beginning to concentrate when it happened again.

"*Now or never!*"

I turned quickly, thinking to catch him before he left. But again, no one was there. Suddenly, as if by revelation, I knew Who it was. There was a Presence in that office which had become very familiar by now. I remembered little Samuel, and how God spoke to him during the night. He hadn't recognized God's voice at first either. But the old priest, Eli, told him, "If you hear that voice again, say, 'Speak, Lord, for thy servant heareth.' "

By now, the Lord had my full attention. "*Now or never*," He repeated. And there was no mistaking what He meant. If I continued on in my engineering career, I would *never* enter the ministry. It was as simple as that.

46

He was asking me to make a choice. And He was asking me *now*.

I was not long in deciding when God spoke so directly and seriously. I answered Him as though He were physically present.

"*Now*, Lord!"

That same day, late in the afternoon, I went to the company president, Mr. Fisher, and told him of my decision. A short time later, I closed the door on that chapter of my life.

When I told Stella that evening her eyes glistened with tears, and all she could say was, "Well, praise the Lord!"

It seemed like a leap in the dark. But I was soon to learn that God is always faithful, and if we walk with Him by faith, any temporary darkness will soon turn to light.

CHAPTER FOUR

Young Birds Fly so High

A few days after quitting my job at Fisher X-ray, Oran Swaback and Bruce Brown from our church came to visit us. They, like us, had been called into the ministry, and for that reason we always had an especially close friendship.

"Andrew," Bruce began, "we've been praying and we feel as though we'd like to go up into Michigan and do some evangelistic work."

"We'd like you to join us," Oran added.

As soon as they mentioned it, it sounded good to me. It seemed like the opportunity Stella and I had been praying for, but I wanted to be sure. I had made mistakes about God's guidance before. So I told them I would pray about it. They, too, understood the importance of divine guidance, and they assured

48

me that they would be praying along with me; then they left.

Stella and I laid the matter before the Lord, and continually asked for His leadership. We talked about it a great deal, and I thought much about the Lord's will for us at that point.

"We've had enough delays," Stella said finally. "If the Lord wants us in His work, then surely He expects us to go through the doors He opens for us."

"But what will *you* do?" I said. The Lord had recently blessed us with a little baby boy, whom we had named John Wesley. I knew it would be impossible for Stella to travel with little Wes.

"I'll stay home," she said. "You go and do what God wants you to do."

Later on we got together with Oran and Bruce, and it was decided that the three of us would form a team and go up into Michigan for a few weeks, but Stella would stay home with the baby.

I had already learned the importance of submitting all decisions to the local church. Since our church had not yet called a pastor, I shared our plans with the presiding elder, Bill Lassen.

"Brother Bill," I began, "you know how Bruce, Oran and I feel called to the Lord's work. We've been praying and we believe the Lord wants us to take a swing up through

Michigan and do some evangelistic work." I searched his face for a reaction, but there was none. I continued, "We're not asking any church to sponsor us. We just feel led to go out witnessing and winning souls for the Lord."

Again I waited. Finally he spoke.

"Andrew," he said with deliberation, " 'Immediately I conferred not with flesh and blood.' "

That seemed like a strange reply! But I remembered the passage to which he was making reference. It's found in the first chapter of Galatians where Paul tells how Jesus called him into the ministry. Paul's call had been so clear and definite that he needed no further advice from anyone. So he said he did not confer with flesh and blood. I saw then that the kindly elder was telling me that if the Holy Spirit had spoken to us about going to Michigan, then we must go and not stop to confer with anyone about it.

I knew it would be hard to leave Stella and the baby; yet both of us were happy that God had opened this door of ministry. She promised me that she would be praying for us constantly.

Michigan was full of excitement. We preached in schoolhouses, town halls and little chapels. Doors opened to us everywhere, and we were busy in services every night. Sometimes the three of us worked together; at other times we split up and had separate services. We had a sense of mission, and it was good to know that we were carrying out the Lord's instructions.

One Friday night, I was scheduled for a service in Big Rapids where we were staying, while Bruce and Oran were to preach in a little chapel quite a distance out in the country. I got back from my service shortly before the other two did and, feeling a little tired, I went to bed. Around 11 o'clock, I heard them coming in.

They were talking about the service they'd had. I guess they thought I was asleep, because they were talking low, like they were afraid they'd wake me up. But I heard every word.

"Shall we tell him?" Bruce was wondering.

"No, let's wait till morning," Oran replied. And they tiptoed into our bedroom, expecting to find me asleep.

"What'd you want to tell me?" I asked, startling them a little. When they saw I was awake, they started in to tell me about their strange experience out in the country.

The little chapel had been packed to capacity. During the service, great conviction had fallen upon the people. The invitation had been given, and the Holy Spirit was plainly at

51

work. Many were coming down the aisle to pray. Sinners and backsliders were beginning to cry out to God, when a certain woman made a move to come down the aisle with the others.

As she approached the front of the chapel, she threw herself to the floor, and went into a spell of some kind, all self-control gone. Those who were praying and seeking God were soon distracted by the commotion she was creating. Bruce and Oran had never seen anything like this before, and didn't know what to do. After awhile, everyone in the chapel stopped praying to see what was wrong with this woman. By this time, the Holy Spirit was quenched, and the service was completely ruined.

I could see that both of them were very depressed about the defeat of the meeting.

"Fellows," I said, "all of us know that God has sent us here to preach the Gospel and heal the sick. But we must not forget that the Bible also says we're to cast out devils."

I paused for a moment to let that sink in. Then I continued.

"Why didn't you take the situation in hand, and cast the demon out of her?"

I knew this was all new to them, so we sat around and talked about it until late in the night. I tried to share with them the little that I knew about the subject.

I finally suggested, "Let's call a prayer meeting. We'll go back out there tomorrow and get the saints together in one of the homes. Then, after we've prayed, we'll go call on this woman and cast the demon out of her." They agreed.

The next morning, we located a Christian friend who was willing to open her home for the prayer meeting. Then we telephoned all the Christian people we knew out in that area, and told them about our plans. After we had made our last call, we wondered what we had gotten ourselves into. None of us knew the first thing about casting out a demon!

About thirty people showed up for the prayer meeting. They prayed fervently, and I sensed the presence of the Holy Spirit in a beautiful way. God seemed to be saying to me, *"It's all right, My son. Your prayers, and the prayers of the people, are heard."*

I stood up and announced what I sensed in the Spirit, and I said to Bruce and Oran, "Let's go to this woman's house. We'll minister to her need, and bring deliverance to her soul." We asked the rest to remain in prayer while we went.

As the three of us were walking out of the room, I noticed an elderly lay preacher in the group. I knew he had lived in that community for many years, had seen many revivals and had been used of God. Before leaving that house, I said to him, "Brother, we'd like to have you go with us to pray for this woman, and cast the evil spirits out of her." Since we were so young and inexperienced, I thought it would be good to have this elderly Christian man with us.

Looking me straight in the face, he said, "Brother Rasmussen, sometimes the young birds fly so high they break their pinions."

I thought that was a strange saying, but I knew what he meant. He admired our faith, but we were not to be disappointed if things didn't happen as we thought they should.

So we went on without him, thankful not to be hindered by his apparent lack of faith on that occasion. Our faith was high. We had prayed, and we were confident that God had answered.

We had learned as much as we could about this woman, and how she came to be in such a miserable state. When she was younger, she had earnestly sought the Lord for salvation, and had started out to live a Christian life. However, her father was dead set against religion of all kinds, and he decided to put a stop to this "foolishness."

"If you get baptized," he threatened, "I'm going to wear this hickory stick out whipping and beating you!"

And he laid the law down so strongly that the poor girl was frightened to death, and didn't dare get baptized. Not long after this, she became interested in spiritualist meetings. Her father didn't say anything about that, so she continued to go to these meetings. Now every time she came into a Gospel service and heard about Jesus and His blood, she would put on some kind of scene, and ruin the service. So I knew there were evil forces at work in her.

When we arrived at her home, I was surprised to learn that she was 60 years old. Her mother lived with her, and was over 80. We began to minister to them as soon as we went in. We took the Bible and explained all about salvation, forgiveness, cleansing, grace, mercy and the power of God. When we finished, we drew up a big breath and asked them if they would accept Jesus. To our amazement, they said they would.

They were very quiet. There was no demonstration or resistance. No ugly scenes such as took place the night before. As the saints prayed back in that home prayer meeting, God was overruling the power of Satan.

We laid our hands upon the woman, anointing her with oil, taking authority over the evil spirits, binding and casting them out, just as the Scriptures declared we should. The woman began to weep. The power of Satan was broken. She gratefully thanked us that we had come and brought the message of salvation to her home. The mother, equally as happy, rejoiced that we had come to make Christ real in her life.

From that day on, this woman came to our meetings and never caused another disturbance of any kind. She was always quiet and peaceful and received the Word of God with appreciation.

As we went back to the prayer group with the news, we rejoiced over the mighty miracle we had just witnessed. Had not Jesus said, "These signs shall follow them that believe; In my name shall they cast out devils ..."? How we praised God for the manifestation of His power! But then we remembered how Jesus sent out His disciples two by two, and how they too had come back rejoicing because the devils were subject to them. Jesus had said, *In this rejoice not, that the spirits are subject unto you; but rather rejoice, because your names are written in heaven.*

It was an important warning to all of us about the dangers of pride. After all, one feather in the cap is all it takes to make some people topple.

CHAPTER FIVE

Miracle in Larsen's Kitchen

"You old devil, get out of here!" The authority of my own voice almost frightened me. But I meant business.

It was a beautiful night; I had decided to spend some time alone with God out in the moonlit fields. I was feeling my need of Him more and more these days. In fact, the longer the three of us ministered in Michigan, the more I became aware of my own inadequacy. The demands of witnessing and preaching every day were beginning to tell on me. I was becoming painfully aware that I needed a special enduement of power.

It was a perfect night to pray. Everything was awesomely silent except for the occasional chink-chink of a night bug who was disturbed by my feet swishing through the grass.

The moonlight filtered down through the dark shadows of the trees, and I wondered if it had been like this when Jesus spent nights in Gethsemane.

I wanted the power of the Holy Spirit more than anything else. As I walked along, I remembered how Jesus had promised, "*Ye shall receive power, after that the Holy Ghost is come upon you: and ye shall be witnesses unto me . . . .*" My mind went back to the prayer experience I'd had in the pastor's study in Chicago a number of years before. Whatever that was, it had been good, but now I was feeling a deep need of something more.

I had read and re-read the accounts of people receiving the baptism in the Spirit in the book of Acts, and there was something about those stories which disturbed me. I had noticed that in every case where the details were given, they had spoken in tongues. It was true on the day of Pentecost. Again in Samaria. And again in the household of Cornelius. The Holy Spirit had taken special pains to record this, and I wondered why. Not only that, but I noticed that every apostle, including Paul, had spoken in tongues. *They* had spoken in tongues, but *I* had not.

"Maybe I've been missing something," I thought to myself. "Perhaps what happened to me in Chicago wasn't really the baptism in the Spirit at all."

The more I thought about it, the more dis-

satisfied I became. As I went out to pray that
night, there was a deep yearning for the fullness of the Holy Spirit. I knew I had to be
careful though. I had heard some weird things
about these "tongues-speakers," and I certainly didn't want to get mixed up in anything wrong. But, on the other hand, if it was
right for the apostles to worship in tongues,
how could it be wrong for me? So I knelt
down and began to pray under the open heavens.

"Jesus," I began, "I need power. Won't you
baptize me in the Holy Spirit as you did the
one hundred and twenty? Won't you baptize
me as you did the apostles?"

A rabbit heard me praying and scurried off
into the woods.

"Jesus," I pleaded, "I need Your power in
my ministry! Won't You baptize me now?"

Just then, another thought popped into my
mind: "Maybe your problem is deeper than
that. Maybe you haven't been born again, after all. Are you really sure?" That was when I
really went into high gear.

"You old devil, get out of here!" I shouted.
There was no question in my mind about it—it
was the devil. I recalled that when Jesus was
tempted, the first suggestion Satan made to
Him was, "IF thou be the Son of God . . . ." I
knew this was one of the devil's favorite tac-
tics—casting doubts on our relationship to

59

God, hoping to drive us into discouragement and confusion.

"I rebuke you, you foul devil!" I kept saying.

"You're not a Christian," he would reply. "You just *think* you are!"

Then I remembered how Jesus had dealt with the devil by using scriptures against him. If it worked for Jesus, it ought to work for me.

"You old devil," I said, "it is written, Jesus 'came unto his own, and his own received him not—but as many as received him, to them gave he power to become the sons of God, even to them that believe on his name'!"

I paused for a moment, as though to let it sink in.

"Now," I continued, getting ready for the assault, "I *have* received Jesus—and I *have* accepted Him as my Savior and the Son of God. Therefore, according to the Word of God, I *am* a son of God. So get out of here, you old devil, and tempt me no more!"

It worked. The tormenting thoughts ceased as abruptly as they had begun. I was never again to be tempted on that question. It was settled forever.

I resumed praying for the power of the Spirit, and kept at it for quite some time. I told the Father in every way I could think of that I needed the fullness of His Spirit. But nothing happened. Finally, I gave up and went home in disappointment. The night that had seemed so beautiful now seemed terribly depressing.

The next evening, I went to see a neighbor by the name of Larsen about coming to the baptismal service on Sunday. Many had been saved in our services and we thought it was important to immerse them as soon as possible. But Brother Larsen was not in a very "objective mood" that evening.

"Brother Rasmussen," he said, "I'm sorry, but I'm not coming. I just don't feel right about what you're doing."

"What do you mean?" I asked.

"Well," he said, "I'm beginning to suspect that you're getting ready to start a new church, and if so, I want you to know I'm not in favor of it."

"My brother," I said, "we're not here to start a church. We're just here to evangelize and baptize believers as Jesus commanded. After that, they can join whatever church they please."

I was trying to be as kind as possible. He was a good man who loved the Lord, but apparently there had been some kind of misunderstanding.

We talked on for quite some time and, finally, I thought I had him persuaded.

61

"Please come," I said.

"Well, I *might* come," he said, "but don't count on it."

I was terribly disappointed.

"However," he added, "can't we have a word of prayer together before you leave?" That was about 10 o'clock.

He too had been seeking the baptism in the Holy Spirit, along with his wife, and I welcomed the opportunity to pray with them. The three of us knelt together in the kitchen and he began to talk to God. About halfway through that prayer, something happened that struck me as uncommon. Suddenly, his speaking became jumbled, and he began stammering* - and making unintelligible sounds.

"What on earth. . . ?" I thought.

He kept it up for a few minutes. Then I became fearful. Visions began to come to my mind of my old pastor and some of the good church people back in Chicago who had warned me about this kind of thing.

"Don't ever go into one of those Pentecostal meetings," they had said. "That's all of the devil. They talk about the baptism in the Spirit, but they don't have it."

I remembered some of those storefront missions in Chicago where they made so much noise, shouting and praising the Lord and having a good time. Everytime I came to one of

*see Isaiah 28:11.

62

those places, I would cross the street to avoid contamination by demons. I was sure they were being controlled by the devil, and I wanted no part of it.

As I knelt there in that kitchen listening to that man stammering in seeming confusion, I wondered why God would permit such a strange thing to happen. I knew the man was an earnest Christian. I knew how diligently he had been seeking the baptism in the Spirit. So why the stammering? I also knew the Lord had promised to give the Holy Spirit to those who ask Him. Was *this*, then, a manifestation of the Holy Spirit?

The very idea seemed preposterous. Yet, knowing that *all* things are possible with God, I had to admit that there was a remote possibility. I had always tried to be very openhearted toward God, and He knew that I was sincere and wanted to know the truth. So, though I felt a little silly doing it, I prayed a prayer, under my breath, so that *no one* would hear me.

"Jesus," I said, "if this is really You, let him speak clearly in a language."

I had no sooner prayed that prayer than he stopped his stammering and began speaking fluently in an unknown language. I had no idea what he was saying, but there was no mistake about it—it *was* a language. Each syllable in each word was being carefully articulated, as I listened in amazement.

He spoke for a long time. I thought I sensed the presence of God, and yet I was afraid. I was troubled at the possibility of being deceived by a counterfeit. I was worried about sanctioning and receiving something that wasn't of God.

"Jesus," I said, still praying under my breath, "please forgive me, but if this is *really* You, give me another sign. Let him interpret what he is saying."

I had read in the Bible that anyone who speaks in an unknown tongue should pray for the power to interpret. And it seemed to me that this would be a great evidence of its reality.

I had no sooner prayed, than Brother Larsen began to interpret! It was a message from the Lord to me. It was so beautiful, and so full of love and tenderness that it melted my heart. As he spoke, he mentioned incidents out of my past which I was sure he knew nothing about. But under the power of the Spirit, he spoke *about* me and *to* me, and every word was true. Immediately I realized that no man could know these things except by the Holy Spirit. God was in that kitchen!

"Jesus!" I cried out, lifting my hands heavenward. "Please baptize *me* with Your precious Holy Spirit!"

Those words had hardly left my lips when the Holy Spirit came down upon me in great power. I tried to praise God in English, but

English words wouldn't come. Instead, words came forth like a torrent in a language I had never before spoken. It was so beautiful I didn't want to stop. On and on I went—ten minutes, fifteen, twenty, thirty, an hour. Something was opening up on the inside of me that felt like a *river* of living water. During this time, I had a vision.

I saw a great auditorium packed with people. I saw them sitting there, awe-stricken by the power of the message. The Holy Spirit was moving upon them to surrender to Christ. I extended an invitation and saw them in the Spirit as they left their seats and poured into the aisles. They streamed down the aisles until there was no more room. I saw all of these people calling upon the Lord for salvation. Oh, what a meeting this was in the Spirit!

But there was more. I began to sing in the Spirit in another language. I sang invitation after invitation, and the people kept coming like the waves of the sea. Another invitation— another wave; another invitation—another wave. For an hour and a half this went on. I found myself wishing it would never stop.

When it was over, I realized that my call to the work of the Lord had been mightily sealed by the baptism in the Holy Spirit. I went home that night a happy, happy man.

*wave. For an hour and a half this went on. I
found myself wishing it would never stop.*

When it was over, I realized that my call to
the work of the Lord had been mightily sealed
by the baptism in the Holy Spirit. I went
home that night a happy, happy man.

CHAPTER SIX

The Blessed Mess

By the time I arrived home, it was 2 o'clock in the morning. Bruce was still rooming with me, and I was sure he would be sleeping. But I was so filled up with the power of God, I knew I would have to tell him.

I tiptoed into the room. Enough light was shining in from the hall so that I could see all right. There he was, sleeping like a baby. I shook him by the shoulder.

"Bruce!"

"Mmmmmmmm . . . ."

"Bruce! Wake up! It's me!"

"Mmmm—yeh, whadyawant?"

He opened his eyes and looked at me groggily. There I was, glowing like a 300-watt electric light bulb!

"Bruce!" I said excitedly, "the Lord baptized me in the Holy Ghost!" That's all I could say. No more English words would come. I began to speak this other language. The words literally tumbled over one another to get out over my tongue.

I can see him yet. He raised up in the dim light on his elbow, looked directly at me and said calmly, "Andrew, that's all of the devil." Then he lay down and went back to sleep.

I didn't blame him. He had been warned the same as I had been, and he didn't understand. But I understood. I didn't go to bed at all that night. I went out to the hayloft in the barn and spent the whole night in prayer.

Bruce's reaction was a mere foreshadowing of problems and temptations to come. Both Bruce and Oran became very cold toward me and my tongues-speaking experience. Any thoughts I'd had about sharing my experience with them were quickly dashed to the ground. They didn't want to discuss the matter at all, and I began to sense that we would have to separate. I was baptized in the Spirit, and saw the work of God from that viewpoint. But Bruce and Oran continued on in the way they'd been trained. So the inevitable happened, and there was a parting of our ways, and I went back to Chicago. I didn't understand it then, but through the years I have learned that each new level of relationship with Jesus involves some degree of separation and misunderstanding. The meaning of Jesus' mysterious words in the tenth chapter of Matthew now became very clear to me:

"Think not that I am come to send peace on the earth: I came not to send peace, but a sword. For I am come to set a man at variance against his father, and the daughter against her mother, and the daughter in law against her mother in law. And a man's foes shall be they of his own household."

(*Matthew 10:34-36*)

When I arrived back in Chicago without Oran and Bruce, I knew there would be some tall explaining to do to everybody. Especially Stella. I hated the thoughts of what might happen between us if she decided to oppose me too, but there was no way to hide it, so I told her the whole story.

She sat and listened in open-mouthed wonder. As soon as I was finished, she went into high gear with a million questions.

"Andrew, I don't understand; I always thought you believed that speaking in tongues was of the devil."

"I did until I experienced it myself."

"But what made you think you needed this?"

69

"The Bible."

"The Bible? Andrew, I don't know what you mean. Where is it in the Bible?" As simply as I could, I showed her all the scriptures God had made so plain to me while up in Michigan.

"You believe you've really received the baptism of the Holy Spirit then?"

"Yes."

"And it happened to you in Brother Larsen's kitchen?"

"Yes, praise the Lord!"

"And tell me again, what was it like?" I again rehearsed all the details that were still so vividly impressed on my mind, and assured her that it was indeed a wonderful experience.

"And if this is really the baptism in the Spirit, then you will have more power in the Lord's work than ever before, right?"

"Right—that's what the Lord promised."

"It's too bad Oran and Bruce didn't understand," she said wistfully.

"Then you don't disagree with me?" I asked anxiously.

"No— I guess not. I don't understand much about it yet; but Andrew, I've never doubted your honesty with God, and if you've received this deeper experience with God, there must be something to it."

"Thanks, Honey," I said, trying to hold back tears of relief. "You're one in a million."

There was a moment of silence. Then she

said, "Well! What do *I* have to do to get this baptism?" I explained it to her as simply as I could, and we prayed together. But nothing unusual happened.

"It's all right," I said. "We'll just keep praying. God will answer."

A short time later, we agreed that it would be wise to change our church membership to the Ebenezer Pentecostal Church, since we were both now committed to an interest in the Spirit-filled life.

"Andrew," the pastor said to me one day, "after all the experiences you've had and the way you've proved yourself in our church, I think you ought to be ordained."

"Ordained!" I think my heart skipped a beat at the mention of the word. I had known for many years that God had already ordained me to the ministry. But every young man in the ministry looks forward to the day when that ordination will be confirmed by the Church.

So it wasn't long until they had an ordination ceremony for me, and I became an officially recognized minister of the Gospel. What a day that was for Stella and me! She was happy as a bird and chattered away until late in the night. Before we fell asleep we both knew that the time had come for us to try our

71

wings of faith, leaving all our earthly sources of income and fully trusting God to supply all our needs. We both agreed it would be an exciting venture.

Stella and I were living in an apartment which we were renting from Emma Wester, the widow of our former pastor. One day I decided to have a talk with Mrs. Wester about the big step of faith we would soon be taking.

"Sister Wester," I said, beaming, "the Lord has been speaking to Stella and me about going full time into the work of the Gospel." I expected her to beam back at me, but she didn't.

"Andrew," she cautioned, "don't jump too quickly. Christian men like you are needed in other professions. I can tell you from experience that it's hard in the ministry, and many trials and testings will be yours. So be very sure before you begin."

"But Sister Wester," I insisted, "I *am* sure. I appreciate your concern for us, but both Stella and I believe that God has spoken to us about this."

"Well," she said teasing, "if you're *that* sure, then there's only one thing to do, isn't there?"

"Yes," I replied. "We're going to sell all our furniture and buy an old car that we can afford. We're going to travel up to Pennock, where I was born, and start a ministry there."

She smiled as though she had a special understanding of my desires. "I know," she said, "but don't forget, you'll need a home to come back to."

"God will take care of that," I said.

We were in Depression days and money was hard to get. Many organizations had gone bankrupt. Many people had committed suicide because of their unbearable losses. A number of years previously I had invested money in real estate, planning for a future home in a nice community. But when the Depression struck, it became almost impossible to make the payments. Besides, there were other debts. Not wanting to enter the ministry burdened down with indebtedness, I decided to let the property go back to the real estate company, and concentrate instead on getting my other bills paid.

"Lord, you know what a mess I'm in," I prayed, "and you know all about the bad financial conditions these days. Even though it seems impossible, I'm asking you to take care of our needs."

Stella and the baby had retired for the night, so it was a good opportunity to wait quietly before the Lord. Not a sound was heard except for the steady tick-tocking of the old clock on the mantel. About 10 p.m., the Lord made something very clear to me.

"*My son,*" He said, "*your prayers are heard; your needs will be met.*"

I thanked Him and went to bed.

A few days later, I received a registered special delivery letter from my father who was still living on the farm back in Minnesota, some 600 miles away. The message amazed me:

Dear Andrew,

A few days ago when I arose to start the fire in the kitchen stove so your mother could come down and make breakfast, I was sitting alone thinking about nothing in particular, when an image appeared to me on the wall. It was like an image on a movie screen.

I saw a highway and I saw you walking on this highway. You were casting off stones to the right and to the left.

I said, "Andrew, what are you doing?"

And I heard your voice just as though you were in that very room with me. You said, "I am casting stones off the highway, preparing it for the people who are to follow."

And then the vision went away. But, much to my surprise, the same vision returned the next morning.

I saw you on the same road. You came to a huge rock on the road which was obstructing traffic. You put your shoulder to it and tried to move it. You pushed and sweated, but couldn't budge it. Finally, you looked down from where you stood and pled, "Come—come and help me!" Immediately, I found myself in the vision beside you, and together we rolled the stone off into the ditch.

I disappeared from the vision, but you continued removing stones and preparing the way for the people who were to follow.

Now here is the help you need to move that rock you could not move alone.

Dad

My hands trembled as I unfolded a check for $600. It was enough to pay every bill I had. Not only that, but there was enough left over to buy ourselves some badly needed clothing. This *had* to be a miracle. In those days when you could neither save, earn nor borrow money, God had opened the windows of heaven and provided for all our needs. I learned that when God calls, He makes a way. I knew this was a confirmation from God that I should not hesitate, but go immediately to fulfill the mission He had given me.

CHAPTER SEVEN

A Prophet In His Own Country

In a short time we purchased an old Chandler automobile, now obsolete (in fact, it was obsolete when I bought it), and prepared to move. It didn't take us long to sell our furniture. In a few days we were heading back to my home town—the little farming community of Pennock, Minnesota. I could hardly wait to get there. All the way back, Stella and I kept talking about the things we were going to do.

From the start, it seemed that we should work with as many churches as possible, accepting whatever speaking engagements the Lord would give us. There were quite a number of churches in the area—the Lutheran Church in which I had been raised, the Mission Covenant Church, the Baptist Church, the Salvation Army and a number of others.

Because the community was small and our family was well-known, I was able to schedule a number of services almost immediately.

The service at the Salvation Army Hall was outstanding. How it warmed my heart when I saw all those people packed into that hall to hear their native son preach the Gospel! When I gave the invitation, so many people came forward there was no room for them all. I remembered my vision in the Larsens' kitchen back in Michigan.

After the service was over, one of the deacons of the Covenant Church, Emil Loven, came to me with tears in his eyes.

"Andrew," he said, "this is the kind of meeting we used to enjoy in the Covenant Church years ago, when God moved so mightily on us."

I was pleased to hear these words from one of my old neighbors who had known me from the day I was born, and to have such a warm reception from so many people. But I couldn't help wondering how they would react when they found out the secret of my power.

Meanwhile the success bubble kept getting bigger and bigger. I'll never forget a service we had one Sunday afternoon in an old schoolhouse. I had prayed the night before that God would pour out His Spirit on the service. When the time came for us to begin, the building was filled, and among them was my Uncle Rasmus, a devout Lutheran. I preached a hard-hitting sermon about sin and the importance of forgiveness. After the service Uncle Rasmus thanked me so warmly that I knew his heart must have been deeply touched. It pleased me to know that even my own relatives were feeling the power of the Holy Spirit working through me. My father and mother were often in the services, as well as my sisters and brothers. I could see that they were proud of me, and I was happier than I had been for years. But just about the time I was beginning to think that the Spirit-filled life was really great, a few complications began to develop.

One of the problems had to do with baptism by immersion. Many of the new converts had inquired about being baptized. They had been very receptive to my teaching and earnestly desired to take this additional step. But, obviously, this would be risky.

"What am I going to do?" I asked myself. "We have Lutherans, Mission Covenanters, and Baptists. Some of their churches teach immersion; others do not. Some baptize babies; others do not."

In the light of the Bible, it seemed that I was obligated to stick my neck out and schedule a baptismal service, regardless of the consequences. Naturally, the Baptist Church was wide open to this suggestion, and I accepted the invitation of the Baptist pastor, Rev. Peterson, to hold the service in his church in

Kerkhoven. But, wanting to avoid any unnecessary confusion, I decided I had better have a talk with the pastor of the Covenant Church, because a number of his people were involved.

"Pastor," I said, "I am sure you understand that I have not come to form a new church."

"Yes."

"Nor have I come to take any people from your congregation."

"Yes."

Clearing my throat, I said, "However, I do have a definite conviction that I must do all that Jesus commands me. I trust that you have no objections to my baptizing some of your members by immersion. We've been studying the Bible together, and they now feel that they should be baptized in that way."

To my surprise, we had a pleasant conversation and he did not object. Yet I wondered about his inner feelings. It seemed strange to me that he should be so cooperative on this highly controversial issue. Since I had done my best to establish an understanding with him, however, I began to look forward to the service with keen anticipation.

When the big day came, the Baptist Church was completely filled, and the overflow crowd was standing in the streets. It was a happy service, and I fairly bubbled over with joy at the privilege of baptizing so many new converts. There were people present from all the

79

churches, and no one seemed to be the least bit disturbed about the immersion issue. So I decided that I had been wrong to be anxious about the matter, and left that service in an optimistic frame of mind. A few days later, however, two deacons from the Covenant Church, Emil Loven and Oscar Hagman, were standing on our doorstep. The first thing I noticed were the tears in Emil's eyes. And the second thing I noticed was the long petition in his hand.

"Andrew," he said, with trembling lips, "I must tell you that our church has taken exception to your ministry, seeing you are baptizing believers by immersion."

I could see that it was very hard for him to tell me this. He had been a neighbor of ours for many years, and I knew him well. In fact, he was related to our family in some way. I knew how hard it was for him to carry out this duty the church had assigned him.

"I have a petition here," he said, handing me the long sheet of paper, "and there are many names signed. It is their desire that you preach in our church no longer. Please understand, these are not our personal feelings, but we must obey those who are over us."

The poor fellows were so shaken that Stella and I felt worse for them than we did for ourselves. We had a pleasant conversation for a while, and then prayed together. When they left our home, we experienced a great welling up of compassion for them. We knew it had been a painful experience for them to go through. It was a bitter disappointment, but I had already learned that when one door closes, God always opens another.

It was not long until a friend by the name of Joe Holmgren came to me and said, "Andrew, my building in the village is open to you as long as you stay here to preach the Gospel of Jesus Christ." So, in spite of obstacles, I was able to go on with the ministry I had begun. But not for long.

I was convinced that the time had now come for me to lead the converts on into the deeper things of God, so I began to teach them about the baptism in the Spirit. It was a great delight to see how readily they received the word of God, and how diligently they began to seek for this deeper experience in Christ. Finally one received. Then another. And another.

Soon the news began to spread, and the opposition from the churches began to mount. Some of the people went to my parents and complained that I was causing division in their churches. As I watched the dark clouds of suspicion and anger looming over my ministry, I thought and prayed much about what I should do.

Certainly, it was not my desire to cause dissension among my friends and neighbors. It seemed quite obvious that my task was done.

I had begun the ministry; now others could step in and continue as directed by the Holy Spirit. So Stella and I packed up our belongings and went back to Chicago.

I knew I would need some temporary employment to tide us over until the Lord directed me to my next assignment. I had been praying earnestly that God would give me some clear direction. Most of the factories were still suffering from the Depression, and there was very little work to be had. But I was confident that God would take care of us.

Remembering a company where I had previously worked for a short time, I decided to go down and re-apply for my old job. When I arrived at their offices, I talked with the chief engineer, Mr. Olsen, and quickly explained my problem to him.

"Mr. Rasmussen," he said, "there is no job. In fact, we laid off two men yesterday." For a moment, it sounded very discouraging. "However," he continued, "even though there is no position open, we're going to *create* one for you, so prepare to come to work tomorrow!"

The next day I was at work, marveling at how God had provided. I had told the Lord I didn't want to run up debts, and that I was depending on Him to help me. He hadn't failed. In a few days, I was receiving my paychecks regularly. But God was not going to allow me to get comfortable in secular work again. After a few months, Mr. Walsh, the chief draftsman approached me. I could see that something troublesome was on his mind.

"Mr. Rasmussen," he said, "I'm sorry, but as you know, these are days of Depression and work is mighty hard to come by. The fact is we have run out of work orders and there is no more work. We will have to lay you off as of tomorrow."

I was hearing more than the chief draftman's voice. To me, that was the voice of God. There was no more work for me there. God had work for me somewhere else. I had learned that God knows when to open a door for employment, and He knows when to close it. It was so in Paul's day. He was a preacher of the Gospel who lived by faith, but there were times when he worked with his hands to provide for himself and for those who worked with him.

My testimony had appeared in *Sannigens Vittne* (Witness of Truth), a Swedish paper which was being circulated among the Scandinavian Pentecostal churches in those days. As a result, I was invited to speak at quite a number of these churches all across America. For a month, I traveled by train from place to place, having special services. As I traveled over the miles, I wondered what God had in store for me. I had the feeling that even those services were only temporary—that God was getting ready to launch me into something else. When I arrived back in Chicago, my hunch was confirmed.

Stella handed me three letters which had come in the mail while I had been gone. Each one was a call to a church! It might have been easier had there been only one letter. But three! That meant I had to get some definite guidance from the Lord. I talked it over with Stella, and spent a good deal of time praying over the matter, and thinking about what I should do. There were various good reasons I could see for accepting each one. There was one idea which kept surfacing as I prayed, however.

"Lord," I said, "I want to take the hardest one, the most difficult one. That's the one that will need my help most."

So I accepted a call to the Bethel Pentecostal Assembly in Tacoma, Washington. This church was a particularly difficult one because it had been a Scandinavian congregation, and all of the services had been conducted in the Scandinavian language for many years. But now they were in the process of transition from Scandinavian to English; it was proving to be a difficult time for them, with many conflicts between the older people who preferred the services in their native tongue, and the younger people who preferred English. Speaking in the Scandinaviah language presented no difficulty to me. Our farming settlement back in Pennock had been made up of mostly Scandinavian immigrants. My father always spoke Danish around the house, and my mother spoke Swedish. And the services of the little Lutheran Church we attended were conducted in Norwegian. As a result, I had learned all these languages, plus English. So the church presented an interesting challenge to me, and I moved our family to Tacoma.

CHAPTER EIGHT

Fire in the Church!

It was in the early part of 1933. I'll never forget the first service in the Bethel Pentecostal Assembly. Not more than eight or ten people showed up, and most of them were over 50 years of age. I thought that things might begin to pick up after it became more widely known that I was there; but the services droned on for months, with very little sign of any increased interest. It was a very discouraging situation. Most of the services were conducted in the Norwegian language and the younger people had left because there were English-speaking churches they could attend, and they preferred to go to church where they understood the language. Not wanting any divisions in their families, some of the parents had followed their children to these other churches. Fewer and fewer Scandinavian immigrants were moving into the area, and it looked like a losing battle. I realized that Bethel Church would die if we continued using the Norwegian language.

I made a firm decision to begin conducting most of our services in English. It took a while for the word to spread, and some of the older people weren't very pleased. But every now and then, some of our former members would visit our services, and they seemed pleased. When they began to see that I was serious about rebuilding that scattered congregation, and that I was concerned about ministering to the younger people as well as the older ones, the seats began to fill up. Eventually, our services were all English except for one on Sunday afternoon; and the time came when even this had to be terminated.

Within three short years, a dramatic change took place. The attendance rose so sharply that in some services there was standing room only. Instead of straggling into church late, they were coming a half-hour ahead of time. It was a time of spiritual revival for us; I knew we were on the verge of a mighty outpouring of the Holy Spirit.

However, this did not come about by mere wishful thinking. Stella and I had set ourselves on a determined course of prayer and fasting. I also asked the people to come to the

87

church for prayer every morning at ten o'clock. As we prayed together, we knew that God was hearing our prayers; we were not surprised on that Friday night when the power of God fell.

Everyone was kneeling in prayer, and I was on my knees on the platform. Suddenly, there came a mighty impact of the Holy Spirit. It felt like an explosion of supernatural power, filling every part of the building. I was lifted up on my feet. Suddenly I saw a vision on the platform. There was a large serpent under my feet; I began to jump up and down on that serpent, and spun my heel on its head.

The people were petrified. They wondered what was happening to me. They couldn't understand why I was jumping up and down and spinning on my heels. They didn't see what I saw, nor did they experience what I was experiencing. Some ran out, while Sister Hunt ran down to the basement and took hold of the pillars of the church in fear. She told me later that it felt to her like the whole building was trembling under the power of God. We had prayed for revival, and I knew this was God's hour of breaking through.

Our attendance began to grow. As a result, it soon became obvious that our building would need some alterations in order to meet our needs. More of the young people began coming to our services. Some of them wanted to play their instruments in the church orchestra, and others wanted to sing in the choir. We needed a whole new platform arrangement. Since one of our young men, John Torgeson, had studied to be an architect, we asked him to draw up some plans for us. After the initial planning was completed, we began looking forward to beginning the project.

I knew it would cost more than our poor people could come up with in those Depression days, but it needed to be done. Somehow, God would provide. But the way He did it was a complete surprise to all of us.

It was just before Christmas. There was a wreath in almost every window, and a holiday spirit was in the air. Stella had been busy baking all kinds of Norwegian cookies and fruitcakes. I had gone downtown to do some Christmas shopping for my family. After purchasing several gifts, I started home, walking back up the hill from the downtown area. Our church was located on that street and I would pass it on the way home. As I came within sight of the church, I saw the sickening sight: flashing red lights—hoses and streams of water—firemen crawling in and out of the broken windows of our church building.

"Oh, God," I cried out fearfully, "there's a fire in the church!"

I began to run frantically. "God," I sobbed

out, "I prayed for fire, but I didn't mean this kind of fire! God, what are we going to do?"

When I arrived, out of breath from my long run uphill, I saw that the fire was already out. The church janitor came running out, with tears in his eyes.

"Pastor," he said, "I don't know what started it. Maybe the chimney got too hot and started a fire in the wall." I opened the door and was horrified at the smoking, charred embers I saw. We both felt we were ruined.

I rushed home to break the sad news to Stella. As soon as I stepped into the house, she knew there was something wrong.

"Andrew, what's happened?"

"The church—" I stammered. "There's been a fire! We're burned out!"

"Oh, no, Andrew!" she gasped. Her face turned pale.

"Get the children and come on down," I said sadly. "You'll have to see it."

"How bad is it?" she asked as we hurried down to the scene of the fire.

"Bad enough," I said. "We're ruined. We can't use the building."

When she saw it, she cried and cried. We all did. I tried to comfort her with words that seemed hard to believe at that point. "Don't be afraid, Honey. Whatever has happened is for our good. We can't see it now, but we're *going* to see it." I wondered within myself if I really believed that.

But God was doing something we didn't understand. Often we are slow to remember that God moves in mysterious ways, and that His ways are higher than our ways.

Pastor Gray of the neighboring Assembly of God Church said to me, "Pastor Rasmussen, I know what a tragedy this is for you. I want you to know that you are welcome to use our facilities, and we'll be glad to share with you in any way we can, so that you can continue with your Christmas activities." Stella and I both wept at such kindness.

But that was not all. Almost immediately, the insurance people began to talk to us about rebuilding the damaged portions of the church. As a result of their prompt services, a new platform was built into church, along with other improvements just as we had originally planned. In a month, we had exactly what we wanted, and God had arranged it so that it didn't cost us a penny! The insurance covered it all.

By that time, the church was more ready for revival than ever. We began having many special meetings, and many converts were added to the church. It was during this outpouring that Stella was finally baptized in the Spirit. And, oh, what joy filled our hearts to know that we were now united in an even

91

deeper way in the work of the Lord. What meetings those were!

·The crowds became so great that we decided to put up a tent, and continue the outreach in that way. God poured out His Spirit; we had great singing, many conversions and great manifestations of the power of God. However, some of the neighbors complained a little about our noisy meetings. One incident in particular stands out in my mind.

I was standing on the platform, just beginning the meeting, when a man brought a young woman into the tent who was all bent over, obviously in great pain. The man brought her straight to the platform, and explained that this was his wife and that she was in need of immediate prayer. Sensing the urgency of the need, I stopped everything and asked the congregation to pray along with me. Laying my hands on her head, and anointing her with oil, I prayed a brief prayer.

"Jesus, let your power flow through this woman right now, and make her every whit whole!"

Instantly, she straigtened up! The people broke out into praising God, and the woman just couldn't contain herself for joy. We had all seen the agonized expression on her face. Now it was gone, and she was rejoicing before us all. There was hardly a dry eye in that tent. It was at the height of all that rejoicing that I saw a policeman walk into the tent.

"What's going on here?" he shouted.

The neighbors had heard all the noise, and one irate neighbor had called the police. It was an embarrassing moment. But only for a moment.

When the woman who had just been healed saw that officer, she ran to the back of the tent, threw herself into his arms and said, "I'm healed, I'm healed, Officer! I'm healed! I was sick; I had great pain! But look at me now— I'm healed!"

I guess he was a little embarrassed. But he began to see what all the excitement was about, and finally he turned and walked out of the tent, shaking his head in amazement.

The next day I was downtown and chanced to meet the lady who had been healed the night before.

"Tell me," I said, "what actually happened to you last night?"

"Why," she said, "I had been to the doctor, and he had told me that my appendix was in very bad condition and that I should be operated on immediately. I didn't know exactly what to do, but my side was very sore, and I knew I would need to make up my mind quickly. I decided to take a step of faith and come to your meeting, even though I was doubled over in pain. And I came in that condition, and thank God, Jesus healed me!"

We rejoiced again at the goodness of God!

Once more He had proven to us that He is a very present help in time of trouble.

God continued to bless the church. Every month, it seemed, there were new victories and new joys. God had been good to me. I thought of all that had taken place since those days over in Michigan. I mused with some delight at the memory of Brother Larsen stammering at the Lord in his kitchen. What a strange beginning for a completely new life for me! I remembered with joy how the Holy Spirit had been poured out upon me. I chuckled to myself as I thought of the expression on Bruce's face when I stood there in our bedroom speaking in tongues. It wasn't so funny then, though, and we had had our share of heartaches. But in spite of all the painful lessons I had to learn, "the lines had fallen to me in pleasant places," and I had come to see that these dear Pentecostal folk were lovely, humble people who adored Jesus.

And now the church in Tacoma. I felt like I could stay there forever, I was so happy. But God had other ideas in mind.

Pastor Dahl stopped by one day. For a number of years, he had been the pastor of the large Salem Scandinavian Pentecostal Church in Brooklyn, New York. As he was traveling through our area, God led him to stop by and visit with Stella and me. He had something to tell us that was to change our course considerably.

"Brother Rasmussen," he said, "I have resigned my church in Brooklyn, and I have come to ask you if you wouldn't consider becoming the new pastor."

It came to me so suddenly that I had not the slightest idea what to say. I had no thought of leaving my church in Tacoma. It would be foolish to leave a church which was prospering mightily under my ministry. At least, that's the way it seemed at that time. But I assured Pastor Dahl that I would make this an earnest matter of prayer.

Now, as you may well know, strange things often happen when we begin to pray! It was not long until God began to show me that it was His will for me to leave my church in Tacoma and go to Brooklyn. It was hard for me to accept at first, but little by little I began to see God's reasoning.

"At what better time could I leave a church," I asked myself, "than when it is healthy and strong and making spiritual progress?"

Finally, I called a meeting of the church elders and deacons and told them of my decision. They just couldn't understand me at all.

"Pastor," they said sadly, "everything is going so well. We've not had it so good for years—the membership is increasing, there's a sweep spirit in all of the meetings and the fellowship between the board members and the pastor is beautiful. We are so happy with you. Why should you leave us now?"

It was hard to explain.

CHAPTER NINE

The Dream that Returned Twice

"There it is!" I announced, pointing to the big, old theater which housed the Salem Church in Brooklyn, New York. I pulled up to the curb on 7th Street and 52nd Avenue and just sat there for a moment, looking at the building. The three boys had their noses pressed flat against the rear windows, staring curiously at "Daddy's new church." (Our family had grown in the past 8 years.)

"Well, it isn't much to look at," said Stella, "but I'm sure the Lord has a reason for sending us here."

On Sunday, we were warmly welcomed by our new flock. It was a much larger congregation than we had had in Tacoma. In fact, it was the largest Pentecostal Church in Brooklyn. After we had been there a short time, we realized with pleasure their continual interest in the work of the Lord. It was a real joy to work with them.

Not long after we began our ministry at Salem, a neighboring church decided to discontinue their services in the little hall where they had been meeting, and come and join us. With this development, our membership increased to the point where our church was completely packed, and we began discussing the possibility of building a new church or purchasing another building with greater facilities.

However, I was soon to learn that the Holy Spirit had put me in this church for some very definite reasons over and beyond this. I knew I needed to have a better understanding of how to build a congregation in God's way. This was even more important than the erection of the material edifice which would house our congregation. And I was soon to embark on some fascinating spiritual journeys which would take me to new territories.

It was 1936. At that time, there was a teaching going around which belittled the idea of church membership. A great many people, and not a few pastors, were saying, "The churches are full of members who are nothing but hypocrites. The churches have rules and disciplines, but nobody pays any attention to them. So what good are they? And what good is church membership? It is nothing more than a form of godliness without the power thereof."

For the most part, these people were sincere, Bible-believing Christians who had become disenchanted with the churches; they had come out of various established churches in search of a fellowship where they could enjoy the freedom of the Spirit.

The more of these people I met, the more I found myself wanting to avoid them. Not that I despised them—but their searching questions about church membership bothered me. I was secretly beginning to wonder if they were not correct. Why should church membership be so important? Did it really matter whether my name was on a church roll? I was a born-again child of God. Wasn't that all that mattered?

I will always be thankful that these questions came to my mind during my ministry at the Salem Church. Our elders and deacons were seasoned men, well established in New Testament doctrine, government and church order. I will always be grateful for the way they encouraged me to search out my answers from the Word of God.

So I began to search the Scriptures to find out whether church membership had any Biblical basis. The first thing I noticed was the unusual prayer which Moses prayed in Exodus 32. He had been begging the Lord to forgive the sins of Israel. "And if not," he went on, "blot me, I pray thee, out of thy book which thou hast written." The fact that arrested my attention here is that *God keeps a book*.

"Isn't that odd?" I thought. "God knows all of those who are His, and yet, for some reason, He finds it necessary to keep a book."

And hadn't Jesus said something very similar to His disciples? I hunted up the verse in the New Testament and there it was in Luke 10:20:

"... *in this rejoice not, that the spirits are subject unto you; but rather rejoice, because your names are written in heaven.*"

"Fascinating!" I thought. "Their names were written down in the book in heaven simply because they were His children."

I continued my search and found mention of the book of life in a number of other verses. I began to realize how carefully God keeps records. If God keeps records, then the practice of record-keeping cannot be wrong! And if we are to build the Church on earth according to the pattern in Heaven, it would seem that we must of necessity keep a book of names.

The more diligently I studied the matter, the more clearly I began to understand the purpose of keeping books. God's book in Heaven is an accurate, up-to-date listing of

100

those who are walking in fellowship with Jesus. But I noticed in Revelation 3:5 the possibility of having one's name blotted out of the book. That made it very clear to me that those who turn their backs on Jesus will have their names blotted out of God's book. I began to see that the book of life is always kept in up-to-date condition.

"But *why?*" I wondered. "Why does God need a book?"

As I studied on, I soon discovered that the book is not for the Lord's sake, but for ours. The book is being written so that all in Heaven, and all at the judgment, might behold in writing that which God already knows.

So I began to see that if books are kept in Heaven for our benefit, then surely the churches are to keep books for our benefit down here. I began to wonder if the sight of a church roll with one's name blotted out might not be used as a very effective tool to bring backsliders to repentance.

Two thoughts began to take shape in my mind: first, that our friends who were denouncing church membership had valid reasons for being disturbed at the hypocrisy they were seeing in so many church members; second, that what needed to be done was *not* to scrap church membership, but rather, to lift it to scriptural levels.

So we began to be very conscientious about membership in our church. We carefully recorded the name of each person who belonged to our church. No one was ever added to that list unless they were born again, living consistently as Christians, and bearing testimony to Christ both in the church and out.

Occasionally, someone would seek membership in our church who was not qualified, and we would have to turn him down. We felt we were responsible under God to thoughtfully examine every candidate. Names of prospective members were announced to the congregation. It was requested that anyone knowing of a reason why a candidate should not qualify for membership communicate with the elders before the next gathering of the congregation. Any information passed along to us was carefully checked out. If the information turned out to be only a false rumor, the individual's name was cleared. If he turned out to be guilty, however, we then visited him in love and meekness and tried to help him get back to God and live a true Christian life. So in either case it worked out for good. When we were convinced that the man was of good Christian character and sound in doctrine, we would then call a special meeting for members only, and extend to him the right hand of fellowship.

Of course, there were some who accused us of being narrow-minded judges, but I remembered how carefully the Jerusalem Christians had dealt with Paul after his conversion, refusing to fellowship with him until they were convinced that his conversion was genuine. And I remembered that it was only after they had received the recommendation of Barnabas that they finally accepted Paul as a born-again Christian. This seemed to indicate that they exercised great caution in receiving members into their fellowship. I was convinced that any local church could save itself a great deal of trouble simply by being cautious about its membership, just as the Apostles were in the New Testament times.

However, I realized that all of our caution would be in vain if we did not keep our books up to date, just as they do in heaven. I had to face the fact that sometimes discipline would need to be administered and names would need to be blotted out. This was painful to think about.

"It would make me feel terrible if we ever had to excommunicate anybody," I thought to myself. But as I studied the Word of God further, I saw that the purpose of discipline is not for the destruction of the child, but for correcting him and making him an honorable child.

The passage in I Corinthians 5 seemed especially to bear out the idea that God expects the Church to deal with sin. It told about a man in the Corinthian church who was guilty of the horrible sin of incest. Apparently the leaders in the church knew about the matter, but they hadn't dealt with him about it. Perhaps he was a man of good reputation and position. Perhaps he was a generous giver. They hated to expose him. But Paul told them that this is exactly what they must do. "Your glorying is not good," he said. "Know ye not that a little leaven leaveneth the whole lump? *Purge out* therefore the old leaven, that ye may be a new lump . . . ." (I Corinthians 5: 6, 7)

I knew what that meant. We were going to have to get serious about church discipline.

"Lord," I said, "Your will be done." It was not long before the sincerity of that commitment was put to a test.

There was a problem brewing. A number of people had told me privately that something was going on. There was a growing group of people in the church who were becoming quite dissatisfied with me. They were saying cutting things.

"It seems to me that a church our size ought to be able to afford a better preacher than that," one had said.

"Where's he getting all these crazy ideas about church discipline?" another was wondering.

"He hasn't visited me since he's been here," another complained.

"Doesn't he ever do *anything?*"

I decided it was time to call the elders and deacons together for a discussion of the problem. So we met on a Monday evening, and I laid the problem before them as simply as I could. We talked and prayed a long time about what we should do. Finally, one of the men spoke up.

"Pastor," he said, "you know we are behind you 100%. I recommend that we put these troublemakers out of the church." The others seemed to agree.

I was hoping there would be another solution. But if this was God's way, I was willing. I wanted to be very careful, though. The Holy Spirit was showing me that untold damage could come to the church if the matter were not handled with great wisdom.

"Brethren," I said, "I think God is speaking to me. And I think He's wanting to give me wisdom and knowledge about how to handle this. If you will just bear with me and give me a little time to pray and further seek the face of God, I know God will show us exactly what to do."

"Very well, Pastor," they agreed, "we'll stand with you in whatever course you feel led of God to take." So we adjourned our meeting and I went home to fast and pray. One night, not long after, the answer came in a dream.

In my dream, I saw a certain business estab-

lishment. The owner, a member of our church, was behind the counter. My assistant pastor, Rev. John Moseid, and I were standing together talking. As we talked, a man came in and bought some paint. He purchased this and walked out, and we were left alone with the owner of the store. For a moment my attention was drawn to the face of the owner. But then the dream was gone. The next morning I got up and thought nothing about it.

The next night, however the same dream was repeated. *Same store. Same owner behind the counter. Same man coming in to buy the paint. Again I noticed the face of the owner.* When I awoke the next morning, I was troubled. When an opportune moment came that afternoon, I sat down with Pastor Moseid and told him what had happened.

He looked at me knowingly, and then said something that sounded like a pronouncement of God. *"Brother Rasmussen, know that this dream is of the Lord, seeing it has returned unto you twice."* Then he went on to mention the experience of Joseph, who had been guided by the repetition of similar dreams. We decided to go down to the paint store I had seen in my dream, and see what would happen.

It was an uncanny experience. The owner was behind the counter. Pastor Moseid and I were standing there talking. While we were talking, a man came in, went up to the counter, bought some paint and walked out. At that point, my attention was again strangely drawn to the owner of the store. I gazed at him for a moment, and then Pastor Moseid and I looked at each other knowingly. Both of us felt a mighty witness of the Holy Spirit.

I was sure we had found the key man to our problem. And this is exactly what I had been looking for. I knew there was a key figure in the whole complicated maze. In fact, I had shared this very thought with our deacons and elders.

"If you cut the tap root of a palm tree," I had told them, "then the whole tree will wither. And if we can just find that one tap root and cut it, then all the rest of our problem will wither and we'll save the church from a split or division."

I looked at the store owner again. I knew we had found the tap root. Quickly, I went to the counter.

"Brother Pete," I said, "I suppose you know about the trouble we're having in the church—the murmuring, complaining about the pastor and so forth."

"Yes," he said, "I've heard of it."

"I figured you had."

"Yes," he said sadly, "it's too bad."

"Brother," I said, with all the courage I could muster, "God has shown me that you are the main cause and the instigator of this problem. And I ask you to repent, not only to me, but I ask you to stand up before the whole congregation on our membership night and tell them you are sorry for what you have done. I'm sure you know that you've led about thirty others astray with you in this murmuring and complaining."

He tried to look shocked, as though he could hardly believe that I would think such a thing of him.

"Oh, Pastor," he said, "I'm not guilty of anything like that. Why, I love you—I wouldn't do anything to hurt you!"

"Then you deny it?"

"Yes, it's just not so."

He tried to be convincing, but I knew that God had given me a supernatural revelation, and I was not about to be talked out of it.

"Well, Brother," I said, "we'll just leave you with the Lord and see what happens." And we left the store.

About four days later the telephone rang and his wife was on the line.

"Oh, Pastor," she said, "please come down immediately! My husband is dying!" I went over to get my assistant pastor and we went down together. When we arrived, we found him in the clutches of a serious heart seizure. He called me to his bed.

"Pastor," he said weakly, "I am the man." Beads of sweat stood out on his forehead. "I am the man," he repeated. "God gave me a dream and I saw myself driving thirty sheep and they were all black; I was trying to get them to go through a culvert but they wouldn't go." He broke down and cried.

"Please forgive me," he said. "I'm sorry that I have been the cause of so much trouble to you and to the church."

"Brother Pete," I said, "it's all right. You've confessed it now and I've forgiven you, and the blood of Jesus will cleanse you. Pastor Moseid and I are going to pray for you." We anointed him with oil, prayed the prayer of faith and left him.

The Lord was good to Pete; in a few days he recovered from the heart attack and was as good as new. When we held our regular monthly meeting, he came as I had requested and confessed his sin before the whole church. He shed bitter tears as he asked their forgiveness—and what a spirit of tenderness swept over the congregation! I forgave, everybody forgave, and Pete was so humble and meek! We were glad to see that he had turned and softened himself toward the will of God and had not hardened his heart. Had he hardened himself, he might have been taken out of this life at that time. But he repented his wrongdoing, working to persuade his friends to get behind the pastor and cooperate with the church. So we were spared the sorrow of having to excommunicate him from the church. We had sweet fellowship with him from that time on.

I knew that all of this had come about because God had faced me with the importance of dealing with sin in the church. I had learned an important lesson.

I remembered the fornicator in I Corinthians 5. "How did the case turn out?" I wondered. I took my Bible and hunted for a while to see if I could find a clue. I finally located it in II Corinthians 2:6-11:

"*Sufficient to such a man is this punishment, which was inflicted of many. So that contrariwise ye ought rather to forgive him, and comfort him, lest perhaps such a one should be swallowed up with overmuch sorrow. Wherefore I beseech you that ye would confirm your love toward him. For to this end also did I write, that I might know the proof of you, whether ye be obedient in all things. To whom ye forgive any thing, I forgive also: for if I forgave anything, to whom I forgave it, for your sakes forgave I it in the person of Christ; lest Satan should get an advantage of us: for we are not ignorant of his devices.*"

So the discipline administered in that case had also been very effective. But severe spiritual sicknesses are usually cured only by very strong medicine. And it had been true in the case of the fornicator. Paul had told the Corinthians,

"*I have written unto you not to keep company, if any man that is called a brother be a fornicator, or covetous, or idolater, or railer, or*

110

a drunkard, or an extortioner; with such an one, no, not to eat."   *(I Corinthians 5:11)*

That was severe, yes; but the purpose of such discipline was not to destroy the individual, but to save him. So the church had acted on Paul's advice, and the man had been excommunicated in order that he might be made aware of his sin, and that the rest of the members might not fall into the same snare. I suppose that had been a painful situation for them to endure, but it worked. And after a period of time, the man thoroughly repented and sought to have his fellowship renewed in the church. They gladly opened their arms to him, and restored him to membership.

Still, I breathed a sigh of relief that we had been spared the pain of actually excommunicating anybody. We had exercised discipline, but God had stepped in before excommunication became necessary. So the Holy Spirit had taught me a vital lesson which proved to be invaluable in the work of building up the Body of Christ. I became firmly convinced that I had discovered an almost forgotten principle of New Testament Church order.

Our six years at the church in Brooklyn went by quickly. The church grew by leaps and bounds after the disciplinary incident with Pete. Our membership climbed to new heights. There was sweet harmony between the pastor and the members. Our missionary work was flourishing, and from every point of view, the church situation was healthy. It was good to minister to such a wonderful congregation.

In November of 1940 I received a letter, inviting me to accept a call to the Philadephia Church in Chicago.

As I was reading the letter, I began to relive the Tacoma experience all over again. The Holy Spirit had taught me some tremendous lessons about building a local church. I was feeling very comfortable in Brooklyn. But I knew that the Holy Spirit must be free to move me at will, so I began to fast and pray for guidance. Within a week, God made it clear to me that it was time to move.

As quickly as possible, I notified the elders of my decision. They received my word with great regret, but they understood that God's hand was upon my life and that I must allow the Holy Spirit to guide me. So I prepared to move. But God had one more great lesson to teach me before I left.

God made it clear that I was not to leave until my successor had been called. There must be no gap between the outgoing and incoming pastors. The Holy Spirit wanted the church to be cared for, and my responsibilities were not over until the new shepherd came on the scene. This made sense. I knew that untended sheep tend to become restless, hungry and discouraged. So I told the church that I would fast and pray until God revealed a successor.

I was sure that God would make His will known in some way. And one day, the answer came, and I had a name to present to the elders.

"I am not expecting you to accept this name immediately," I said to them. "All I ask is that you pray and ask God for His mind on the matter. In a week, we'll meet together again and see how you feel about it."

I felt this was a scriptural thing to do. If the elders reacted favorably, then it would be brought before the whole church in the same manner, and much prayer and fasting would precede the actual decision. I noticed in Acts 15:22 that when an important decision was made in the apostolic church, it "pleased . . . the apostles and elders with the whole church . . . ."

A week later, I received a favorable response from the elders, and the matter was taken before the congregation. I explained to them the great importance of a prayerful decision.

"You know how important this is," I said, "so let's pray until we know what God wants in this situation. In two weeks, we'll meet again for a vote of affirmation. If the vote is favorable, then I will appoint this man to be your next pastor."

My decision to appoint my own successor had come out of a careful study of New Testament methods. I noticed that the apostles never allowed a church to go untended. I had read in Acts 14:23 that Paul and Barnabas "had ordained them elders in *every church*, and had prayed with fasting . . . ." So the New Testament pattern seemed quite clear: outgoing apostles did not leave a church until they had first appointed successors to continue the ministry.

So it seemed logical to me that an outgoing pastor ought to be responsible for the appointment of his successor. Why not? If the pastor loves God and loves his flock, then he ought to be in a position to appoint the next shepherd. He knows the church operation, he knows the general spirit of the congregation, he knows their needs, and he ought to be able to get God's guidance on the matter of his successor.

On the night that the church met together for the vote, only one man came to dissent. But he said, "As I came to the church and was opening the door, the Holy Spirit spoke to me and said, 'No—the man I have chosen is the one whom the pastor and the elders have indicated.'" So there was a unanimous vote, and Rev. Harry Ring became the pastor of the church.

114

"Praise the Lord for His guidance!" I said to the congregation.

They responded with a resounding "Amen!"

CHAPTER TEN

Removing Spots and Wrinkles

My convictions about church discipline were confirmed in an even more dramatic way in my next church.

Ole was an admirable young man who had been active in the Philadelphia Church in Chicago for a number of years. He was well liked by all of our young people, and we had high hopes for him.

He had been dating Mary for quite some time. She was a sweet Christian girl, and we had been expecting to hear the wedding bells almost any day. One day the two of them came to the church and wanted to talk with me privately. I took them into my study, and closed the door.

"Pastor Rasmussen," Ole began hesitatingly, "we have a terrible problem."

"Well, the Lord is able to solve every problem," I began.

"But it's not that kind of problem," Ole interrupted. He paused for a while, as though he were trying to gather up enough courage to say it. "Mary's going to have a ... a baby ...." He broke down and cried. "We've committed a terrible sin," he continued. "We're going to get married, but it won't be long until everybody will know what we've done."

"What are we going to do?" Mary asked hopelessly. They both sat there, weeping and heartbroken. I couldn't help feeling a deep sense of compassion for them. But regardless of my feelings, I knew there was only one right thing to do. I remembered again the discipline meted out against the fornicator in I Corinthians 5—and here was a couple involved in fornication. I knew I could not afford to take the matter lightly. For even though it was only one young couple that seemed to be involved, yet I knew that it would not be long until the whole church would know. The church, and especially our younger people, were bound to be influenced by the way we handled this problem.

"I'm sorry," I said, "but in the light of the Word of God, we must deal with this problem. I'm very sorry that you two must suffer under this discipline, but I'm sure you understand that I must follow the Word of God."

"Yes, sir."

117

"No chastisement is pleasant," I continued, "but afterward the blessings of God will accompany it. And in the light of what the two of you have told me, it is going to be necessary for me to excommunicate you from the church, exactly as was done in I Corinthians 5."

At that, they both buried their faces in their hands and wept bitterly. It was hard to go on, but after they had quieted down a little, I continued.

"I hope you understand," I said. "If we do not deal with this problem, other couples will be encouraged to commit the same sin, and this must not happen. The rest of the members must learn to fear God and not fall into the same snare of the devil."

They nodded their heads in assent.

"This does not mean that we don't love you," I went on. "We *do* love you both very much, and we're going to pray for you both. If you stand fast in the Lord during this period of chastisement, you will become a blessing and a help to the church in the future."

They seemed to agree with me, but I wondered what the final result would be. Wanting to be doubly sure that they understood, I went on to explain the significance of what I had done.

"The fact that you are excommunicated does not mean that we do not want you to come to church. We want you to come to church faithfully; but because you are excommunicated, you cannot have any active part until you are fully restored to the church again. We're not doing this to destroy you; we're doing it to help you. And we're doing it to help others in the church."

"We understand, Pastor," they answered.

I breathed an inward sigh of relief.

A few days later, I called the elders together and explained the problem to them. When I explained how I had handled the situation, they agreed that I had done the right thing.

On membership night, the whole church gathered together for a meeting, and I told them what had happened: how I had met with the elders, and what our decision had been. I explained that we now wanted a confirmation of the church's desire to stand with the pastor and elders in this action. So they all stood to their feet, except for one person who was so overwhelmed with carnal sympathy for the young couple that she just couldn't bring herself to do what she knew was right. Nevertheless, we felt we had taken the right action in God's sight. Though it made us sad, it was heartwarming to hear how the whole church prayed so earnestly for this young couple that God would give them grace and mercy and, in due season, restore them into full fellowship with the Body of Jesus Christ.

The next day Ole and Mary were officially notified that they were no longer members of our local church. We kept praying for them though, asking that God's mercy would be extended to them and that they would live Christian lives and become good examples to each other and to the church as a whole. Stella was a real angel of compassion during those days, and did everything she could to show Ole and Mary how much we loved them.

Any misgivings we might have had about our action soon gave way to sheer joy. It was working! Instead of being driven away from the church, Ole and Mary continued coming to church. They manifested such a spirit of humility that we finally had another elders' meeting and decided that they had proven their true state of repentance, and that the church ought to forgive them even as Christ had forgiven us, and receive them back into membership.

By this time they were married and living together as a Christian husband and wife. When we took them back into the church, there was great joy as we prayed together for God's blessing upon them. Afterward, we gladly extended the right hand of fellowship to them, knowing that all their past was under the blood of Jesus. In the years to come, they became a great blessing to the church.

The whole incident had a wonderful effect on the congregation, and especially on the youth. They began to develop a far healthier frame of mind. Oh, how they feared God after that and respected His Word and wanted to live right! I saw that it always pays to obey God, no matter what risk might be involved. The Lord wants a clean Church. I remembered Paul's beautiful words in Ephesians 5:25-27:

". . . Christ also loved the church, and gave himself for it; that he might sanctify and cleanse it with the washing of water by the word, that he might present it to himself a glorious church, not having spot, or wrinkle, or any such thing; but that it should be holy and without blemish."

Here was clear teaching about how to remove spots, wrinkles and blemishes from the Church. Spots are to be washed out. They must be removed. At first, I thought the word "spot" referred merely to the spiritual imperfections of the people who make up the Church. But then it occurred to me that perhaps the "spots" spoken of are *people* who have fallen into sin. My thoughts were confirmed when I turned to II Peter and read the Lord's pungent description of certain people in the church:

"Spots they are and blemishes, sporting

121

*themselves with their own deceivings while
they feast with you; having eyes full of adul-
tery, and that cannot cease from sin; beguiling
unstable souls . . . ."*   (II Peter 2:13, 14)

Now I saw it. The spots referred to are
people. And these people who "spot" the
church are to be *washed out*. But how? I went
back to Ephesians again and there it was:

*". . . Christ also loved the church, and gave
himself for it; that he might sanctify and
cleanse it with the washing of water by the
word."*   (Ephesians 5:25, 26)

So it is the *application* of the Word of God
which results in this washing process. And this
is precisely what God had been trying to
teach me. The washing process may be a difficult experience, but the application of the
Word of God always brings favorable results.
We had dared to apply the Word of God and
"wash out" some spots and blemishes. And
because it had been done in the Spirit of
Christ, it worked. Of course, washing always
produces wrinkles. There had been wounded
feelings and broken hearts. But because the
offenders were excommunicated with such tenderness and love, they were finally restored to
the church, and the Holy Spirit pressed out
all the wrinkles!

CHAPTER ELEVEN

A New Move of the Spirit

In two short years I finished up my ministry in Chicago and prepared to move up into Canada. Little did Stella and I know about the amazing things that would happen to us there.

Though I was unaware of it then, miraculous happenings were taking place in many spots all over the world. God was getting ready to move into the days of the last great outpouring of the Holy Spirit upon the Church. The last chapter was about to be written. None of us understood what was happening, though. In fact, it was quite a while before my eyes were opened, and I began to understand what was taking place.

God had been speaking to me for quite some time about developing a church and training center somewhere up in Canada. There were many independent churches which needed to be drawn together into some form of fellowship, and a Bible institute was needed for training young men and women who wanted to devote themselves to the Lord's work. While serving my churches in the States, I had made several trips up to Alberta for speaking engagements, and had finally become convinced that Edmonton was the logical place to begin my work. It was the capital city of Alberta, and the fastest growing city in Canada.

As I waited before the Lord for guidance, little by little my plans began to take shape. The churches at Tacoma, Brooklyn and Chicago promised me financial support. Through the help of a business friend, I was able to find a house for my family just outside the city limits of Edmonton. I made a down payment on it and went back home, convinced that the time had come for us to make the long move.

I knew my task in Canada wouldn't be easy. To be the pastor of a well-established congregation is one thing, but to build a congregation from the ground up is quite another. In Edmonton, there was nothing awaiting me except a few interested people and a hall we could rent for our meetings. But Stella and I were convinced that this was what God wanted us to do.

The trip to Edmonton was trying and exciting. We had built a four-wheel trailer to tow behind our 1936 Ford. This was during World War II, when gas and tires were hard to come by. After the trailer was loaded, the tires were groaning under the pressure and looked half flat, even though we had put in all the air they would hold. Everything we owned was on that trailer—heavy oak furniture, beds, mattresses, rugs, dishes and the stove. And the tires were used. (It was practically impossible to get new ones.) A 2,000-mile trip lay ahead of us, and many dirt roads, detours and chuck holes that we knew nothing about.

When the last piece was in place, I pulled down the tarp and said, "Well, Stella, what do you think?"

She looked at the load in disbelief. I looked at my older brother, Albin, who was standing there surveying the situation.

"I don't know, Andrew," he said, shaking his head skeptically. "You've got an awfully big load there." How well I knew it!

As we started out of Chicago with Wes, Phil, Dave and Jon jammed into the back seat (we had gained another son by that time), we soon found that our home-made trailer was far from perfect. It swayed from one side to the other behind our little old Ford that already had almost 100,000 miles on it. We could only pray and hope for the best. At times, we slowed down almost to a crawl, in order to keep our trailer from weaving too much. But once we got out of the city, it didn't seem too bad.

We were rolling along happily, when Wes, our oldest son, shouted, "Dad! A tire just blew out!"

I had heard the bang, but was hoping that maybe it was just a backfire. But when we pulled off the road, sure enough, one of our tires was flatter than any tire I had ever seen before.

"Oh, well," I said, "we have a jack and some tire patching equipment. We'll soon fix that!" So the boys all got out, eager to help.

"Here, Dad," Wes said, "here's the handle for the jack."

By this time Phil had the patch kit opened. Anxious to help and get some praise for it, he said, "Daddy, here's a good patch. Will this do?"

Jon was the critical and observing type, and was interested in one of the other tires. "Oh, Daddy!" He exclaimed. "I hear something like a bee going Z-Z-Z-Z-Z-Z-Z! It's here on the bottom of this tire. Do you think we've stopped on top of a bumble bees' nest?"

Dave went to see what was wrong. "No, no, Daddy!" He said excitedly. "There's a crack in this tire, and air is coming out!"

About that time, Stella jumped out of the Ford and said, "Oh dear! It never rains but it pours!"

Finally we started on our way again. But this was just the beginning. Before we arrived in Edmonton, we had to stop for eighteen tire repairs.

From Chicago to New London, Minnesota, was 500 miles. Stella's Uncle Martin and Aunt Annie lived there, so we stopped off for the night. Martin was a good mechanic, and the next day he bolted a couple of steel bars onto our trailer to give strength to the steering frame. This completely solved our weaving problem, and we went on our way, happy for Martin's kindness.

When we crossed the Canadian border, it started to rain. There were many detours which took us off onto dirt roads, and we slowed down almost to a turtle's crawl. Eight after days after leaving Chicago we finally arrived in Edmonton.

When we pulled into the dirt driveway of our new home, it was pure mud. The steady rains had turned everything into sticky clay, and I felt the tires of our little Ford sinking down into the ooze. I stepped on the gas, and tried to spin my way in far enough to get the trailer off the road. But it was no good.

Stella got out of the car to see how badly we were stuck, and when she tried to lift her foot, the gumbo pulled her shoe off.

"Oh, Andrew!" she moaned. "Why did we ever come here?" I was wondering the same thing, but didn't say so. We had to leave the car and trailer stuck in the mud. We managed to squish-squash our way up to the house with a few belongings, unlocked the door and got a fire going in the fireplace.

It was a miserable beginning, but we were soon to find that we had warmhearted friends who called on us and brought us food. Later we learned how truly the Lord had given them to us and us to them to build His house and a center of evangelism and missions to the world.

Our first meeting was held in Orange Fraternity Hall. I had publicized the meeting by advertising in *The Edmonton Journal*. A dozen people showed up for the meeting. It wasn't a very impressive beginning, to be sure, but I knew that prayer, patience and hard work would bring results in due time. We had tent meetings and special revival meetings in theater buildings; we used every other means we could think of to make an impact on that city and build a New Testament church.

In 1944, we organized the church with twenty members, and began meeting in the Social Credit Hall. It was a great joy to watch this "baby church" grow. I was careful to feed it a good diet—starting with "milk," but gradually moving on to spiritual "meat."

I thank God that He gave me good elders and deacons who were in full harmony with the teachings of the Word of God and who had a sincere interest in helping me in my ministry. The membership increased and we had beautiful harmony, from the elders right on down through every member in the Body.

"Brother Rasmussen," the elders said to me one day, "we think it's time to start looking for a piece of property, don't you?"

"Yes," I said, "and I have a plan in mind. Let me go talk to the city officials and see if they're willing to deal with us." I felt it would be advantageous for us to purchase city-owned property, because of their policy of giving fifty percent off to churches.

So in August of 1945 we purchased a nice corner lot of 95th Street and 103rd Avenue, and erected a temporary building on it which would house both the church and the Bible school.

By 1946, the church was doing so well that we all thought it was time to begin our Bible school project; so we began to purchase books and search for a competent faculty. The classes would be held in the church auditorium. We publicized the project in many different ways; in that same year, a "baby Bible institute" was born under the sponsorship of her two-year-old sister, Edmonton Gospel Temple.

I can never begin to tell you what a profound influence our Bible school students had on the church. What a zealous group of Christians they were! And how they prayed! Almost continuously, they were asking God for an outpouring of the Holy Spirit. In a short time, I observed a significant development.

Suddenly, they all became interested in fasting. Prayer alone was no longer sufficient; fasting was also necessary. They were in dead earnest about "praying down the power." Oh, what weeping, what heart searching, what pleading went on in those days! The dining room was strangely empty. Prayer had become more important than food.

"Brother Rasmussen," the school chef said to me, "I hardly know when to get a meal ready these days!"

"Well, Alec," I told him, "I think it would be sufficient to keep a large pot of soup boiling on the stove, and they can just help themselves when they get hungry."

"Good idea!" he replied happily. And for the next ten days, those who were hungry would help themselves to a piping hot bowl of moose bone soup.

Most of them wanted to fast, though. Some fasted a day, some three days, some ten days. I remember one who fasted over thirty days. Of course, I was very concerned that no one should go overboard, and it was also of great concern to me that they should know how to break a fast. We secured some literature on the subject and studied it together so that no one would suffer any ill effects.

Reverend T. E. Crane, my associate pastor and president of the Bible school, was a tremendous help to us during those days, along with his wife, Violet, who was our dean of women. Together, we learned much about the blessings of fasting, and how the mind and spirit became more alert and responsive to God during a fast. We were careful, though, never to *urge* anyone to fast. There was always the possibility that some might not be physically able, and any fasting that took place was entirely voluntary.

We learned to exercise special care about long fasts. The first three days were always the most difficult; after that, we lost our habit-hunger, and began to feel stronger. We also learned the value of drinking warm water, since the body becomes rather cool during a long fast.

Breaking the fast required special attention, too. We learned that it was best to eat nothing but thin broth on the first day after a long fast. On the second day, a few easily digested vegetables could be added to the broth. From that point on, we could very gradually build back to our normal eating habits. We found it quite necessary to instruct our students carefully along these lines, so intense was their interest in fasting and prayer.

I knew this was something unusual. But what I did not know was that the same thing was being duplicated in many other areas of Canada and on down through the States. All over North America, the Holy Spirit was brooding over God's people. Hundreds upon hundreds of Christian people simultaneously began to have the unexplainable urge to fast and pray. I was familiar with Joel's prophecy regarding the outpouring of the Holy Spirit in the last days. But I had not noticed how fasting was related to this outpouring. Needless to say, I was somewhat amazed when the Holy Spirit let me "see" those verses:

"Therefore also now, saith the Lord, turn ye even to me with all your heart, and with fasting, and with weeping, and with mourning . . . .

Blow the trumpet in Zion, sanctify a fast, call a solemn assembly . . . ." (Joel 2:12, 15)

A few verses later, my eyes fell on these familiar words:

"And it shall come to pass afterward, that I will pour out my spirit upon all flesh; and your sons and your daughters shall prophesy, your old men shall dream dreams, your young men shall see visions: and also upon the servants and upon the handmaids in those days will I pour out my spirit." (Joel 2:28, 29)

I marvel now as I look back over those days when the Spirit was beginning to move upon us. We had no idea what the outcome would be. We only knew that we felt a strange sense of urgency to fast and pray. We only saw that the Church all over the world was sick, weak, palsied and anemic. Little did we know of God's plan to restore His power to the Church. We were familiar with the Bible teaching that Jesus might return at any time, but we failed to see that He is coming for a healthy Church, full of the Spirit, full of grace, exercising all of the nine gifts of the Holy Spirit (I Corinthians 12:8-10), being perfected by the five-fold ministry gifts (Ephesians 4:11-13) until the Church comes to the fullness of the stature of Christ—a glorious Church without spot or wrinkle. We saw none of this—but we prayed under the guidance of the Holy Spirit.

It was at this same time that the Holy Spirit initiated many unusual ministries all across North America. Oral Roberts began his tent crusades, with mighty miracles of salvation and healing. The great Billy Graham Crusades were also launched during this same period. The Kathryn Kuhlman ministry began in Pittsburgh, with the power of God falling on packed auditoriums. T. L. Osborne traveled around the world in great evangelistic and healing campaigns. The late William Branham took his healing crusades to practically every major city on the continent. Something was happening. The power of the Spirit was beginning to fall.

CHAPTER TWELVE

Power Flowing through Human Hands

One day, after one of our classes, Alvin Isrealson, one of our students, came to me with an interesting suggestion. "Brother Rasmussen," he said, "how would you like to go with me to visit a Bible school over in Saskatchewan? I hear there is a moving of the Holy Spirit over there, too."

When I talked it over with Stella, she agreed that I ought to make the trip, even though this would mean that she would be alone with the children over the Thanksgiving holiday. She knew God was at work in our Bible school, and she felt it would be good for me to get together with other brethren and compare notes. I had never met anyone from the school in Saskatchewan, but Isrealson had attended this school for two years before enrolling in ours. I agreed to go with him.

We left Edmonton at 4 p.m. and arrived at our destination around 7 the next morning—just in time for breakfast. After I was introduced to President Arthur Bensen and his brother Jon, along with some of the other school leaders, we sat down to eat together. Before we left the breakfast table, President Bensen invited me to speak in their chapel service, which would begin at 9 o'clock. I was tired from the night's travel, but gladly accepted the invitation.

"Lord," I said, a few minutes later in my room, "what am I going to speak to these people about? I've just met them; I don't know exactly what they teach or what they believe."

"Speak to them about the Church," the Lord seemed to say. *"Share with them what I have taught you out of My Word about the administration and government of the local church."*

"Well," I thought, "they might as well know what I believe, whether they agree or not." And off I went to chapel, confident that the Holy Spirit would guide me. Little did I know how much I would learn that day.

I always enjoy teaching about local church

order, and when my time came to minister, I started in with a great deal of enthusiasm. I talked about the qualifications for membership in the local church, the importance of church discipline, the administration of the church by the pastor and elders, and the importance of the deacons' sharing in the oversight of the flock.

At first they watched me with some evident curiosity. I had learned by that time that a preacher is never under closer scrutiny than when he speaks to a group of ministerial students. After a while, though, their curiosity about the speaker turned to deep interest in what I was saying. At certain times, their eyes seemed glued on me. At other times, they listened in open-mouthed wonder, and I marveled at their rapt attention.

Immediately after the service, President Arthur Bensen took my hand warmly and said, "Brother Rasmussen, won't you speak to us again this afternoon?"

I was surprised, but agreed to do so. After lunch, the whole day was thrown open to me to minister, and I did it with gladness. I felt a great anointing of the Holy Spirit upon me, and took great liberty in teaching the Word of God. They *drank* in every word.

Afterwards, Al Handlin, one of the teachers of the school explained to me why the teaching had been received so eagerly.

"Brother Rasmussen," he said, "you surely

have brought an answer to our need at this hour."

"How's that?" I inquired.

He went on to relate a fascinating story. For some time, President Arthur Bensen's brother Jon, had been exploring the Bible teaching about the ministry of laying hands on others. The fact that Hebrews 6:1, 2 named this practice as one of the fundamental elements of the Christian faith, side by side with repentance and faith, seemed especially intriguing to him.

"This is exciting!" he thought to himself. "Maybe this is an area of thought which needs to be investigated in more detail."

Not that the ministry of laying on of hands was anything totally new to him. He was very familiar with this little ceremony, and had done it many times himself—in ordination ceremonies, or when prayer was offered for the sick, or when a baby was dedicated to the Lord.

He also knew that the idea of laying hands on others was threaded throughout the entire Bible. In the Old Testament, Jacob laid his hands on Joseph's sons to bless them. Later on, the people of Israel were taught to lay hands on their sacrifices. They also laid their hands on the Levites when they were consecrated to the service of God.

In the New Testament, it was practiced just as widely. Jesus laid His hands on children and sick people. Peter and John laid hands on the Samaritans when they received the Holy Spirit. Ananias laid his hands on Saul so that he might receive his sight and be filled with the Holy Spirit. Jon knew there was no question about it. The practice occupied a prominent place in the teachings of the Bible.

"Strange, though," he thought, "that a practice which was apparently so important in the minds of these Old and New Testament people should now be considered a mere formality by so many modern Christians. I wonder why . . . ."

The more Jon studied the subject, the more fascinating it became. Apparently, every person in Biblical times who practiced the laying on of hands believed that it was in their power to *transfer* something from themselves to another person. New Testament Christians seemed especially confident that the Spirit of God which was *in* them would work *through* them to transfer some particular blessing to the one on whom they laid hands.

"What an interesting thought!" Jon said under his breath. He could almost visualize the power of God flowing down through someone's arm and out through his hands and fingers into the life of another.

But the verse that arrested his attention more than any other was I Timothy 4:14. To be sure, Jon had read that verse many times before, but this time it stood out in bold relief:

"*Neglect not the gift that is in thee, which was given thee by prophecy, with the laying on of hands of the presbytery.*"

"Can you imagine!" mused Jon in disbelief. He ran his index finger along the line and read it again: "Neglect not the gift—which was given thee by prophecy—with the laying on of hands."

Two things dawned on him at once. First of all, the gift which Timothy possessed (whatever it was) was *given* to him when the leaders of the church laid hands on him. Secondly, prophecy had something to do with it. Apparently, there had been a prophetic utterance of some kind by one or more of the elders, indicating what kind of ministry Timothy was to have.

"Hmmm," he thought, "I wonder if I can find anything else on that?" Noting a center-column reference, he flipped back a couple of pages to I Timothy 1:18. There, at his fingertip, he read these words:

"*This charge I commit unto thee, son Timothy, according to the prophecies which went before on thee, that thou by them mightiest war a good warfare.*"

So there it was again. This made it clear that there was more than one prophetic utterance given when the elders laid hands on Timothy, conferring upon him the gift which

God wanted him to have. Jon closed his eyes for a moment; it was almost as though he could see what had happened. He saw young Timothy kneeling, while a group of godly leaders of the church stood around him with their hands on his head.

"Thus saith the Lord," began one of them, "I have set you apart, son Timothy, that you might teach My Word to My people."

Another took up the prophecy. "Yea, I am imparting, through My Spirit, the special ministry of teaching, and from this day you will be My instrument, committing My Word to faithful men who shall be able to teach others also."

Another continued, "Do not hesitate because you are young. The gift I am giving you will make you fully adequate for the ministry of teaching. Be not afraid."

Jon smiled to himself. It was a whole new idea—this link between the laying on of hands and the prophetic conferring of a gift upon another person. In fact, it was such a new idea to him that he began to search the Bible even more intensely for more information. It wasn't long until he found Paul's words to Timothy in II Timothy 1:6:

"Wherefore I put thee in remembrance that thou stir up the gift of God, which is in thee by the putting on of my hands."

So Paul was there too, when this gift was conferred on Timothy! Apparently Paul was

141

saying that Timothy's gift was given at the
precise moment when he and the other elders
had laid their hands on Timothy. The Holy
Spirit, which was in Paul and the others, had
transferred special power into Timothy for a
special ministry.

Jon slapped the desk and said right out
loud, "Lord, I just don't understand it. What
right does any Christian have to impart spiritual gifts to another Christian? Show me another verse!"

It wasn't long until he found Romans
1:11, where Paul says to the Romans, "For
I long to see you, that I may impart unto you
some spiritual gift . . . ."

"There it is!" he said. "Paul actually
thought he could impart spiritual gifts to
other people! And so did the church leaders!
But how could any Christian know what gift
another Christian ought to have? How did
those elders know what gifts to confer upon
Timothy?"

Like a flash of revelation the answer came:
the word of knowledge! Jon quickly leafed
through his Bible until he came to I Corinthians 12:8. There was the list of the gifts of the
Holy Spirit:

*"For to one is given by the Spirit the word
of wisdom; to another the word of knowledge
by the same Spirit."*

Of course! If the Holy Spirit can give wisdom, then He can also give *knowledge* of His

will. He could reveal what gift a Christian ought to have, and he could use another believer to confer that gift through the laying on of hands. And if this was done in the early church, then why not today?

"This is dynamite!" he whispered to himself. And, like dynamite, he knew his discovery could be either a blessing or a curse. He could immediately see the danger of wrong guidance being given. What if some young, inexperienced Christian were to lay hands on another and confer a "gift" which wasn't genuine? Think what frustration and confusion might come to the recipient of such a false prophecy. On the other hand, if it were done prayerfully and under the guidance of the Holy Spirit, think what blessing could come to the Body of Christ from having members who understand their place in the ministry of the Church!

Through the days that lay ahead, Jon began to see more and more clearly that such a conferring of gifts, under the guidance of the Holy Spirit, might trigger a great restoration of gifts which had seemingly been lost to the Church. It might also be the means of awakening the Church to the importance of ministering one to another, instead of the traditional "one-man-show" of most denominations.

Take Milford Kirkpatrick, for instance. Mil was one of the young teachers at the Bible school. Jon had often found his mind turning to Mil as he meditated about this matter of conferring gifts. He was certain that God had his hand on Mil for some particular kind of ministry.

"I wonder what would happen," Jon thought, "if I would lay my hands on him and prophesy . . . ."

That was a frightening thought. Mil was a well-balanced Christian. He loved the Lord. It would be tragic to give him any wrong guidance. Jon wanted to dismiss the idea, but still it kept returning. So he decided to make it a serious matter of prayer.

Nobody knew what had been going through Jon's mind on that eventful day when they gathered for the school chapel meeting as usual. Jon couldn't get the idea about Mil out of his mind. He wanted to forget it. It was a crazy idea anyway. But all those Bible verses . . . .

It was then that Mrs. Knudsen, one of the women students, stood up and said something strange. Looking straight at Jon, she said, "My servant, what the Lord has asked you to do, *do it*, and be not afraid." Then she sat down.

Jon knew that message was for him. Rising and moving to the front seat where Mil was seated, he took Mil's hand.

"What's this all about?" Mil wondered to himself.

"Mil," Jon began, "thou art a servant of God . . . ."

"He's prophesying!" Mil thought.

"And I say unto you, you are a chosen vessel unto Me and you shall be My apostle . . . ."

"Apostle? Me?" (He didn't understand at that time that apostles are roughly equivalent to missionaries.)

But Jon went on—and on. For over half an hour he prophesied about Mil's ministry. He also went on to prophesy about the outpouring of the Spirit and the restoration which was coming to the Church. Mil sat there in awe, remembering how the power of God had come down on him just the night before, and how God had dealt with him about his place in the Body of Christ. How could Jon have known?

But nobody knew how Jon was struggling. An accusing voice within him said, "Boy, you've really done it now! Here you've gone and made Mil an *apostle!* How could you have done such a dumb thing?"

Everybody else was confused too. Nobody there had ever seen such an old manifestation, so they finally agreed to take three days off for fasting, prayer and searching of the Word. Every student and every member of the faculty earnestly sought God's guidance. If this manifestation was of God, they certainly didn't want to fight it. But if there was an error, they knew it had to be corrected.

145

They examined every passage of Scripture they could find on the subject. They meant business. At the end of the third day, they all agreed that what Jon Bensen had done was perfectly scriptural. Not one person disagreed. They were convinced that this was a scriptural use of the laying on of hands.

However, they all saw the possible dangers. And they quickly saw the importance of caution and extreme reverence in the handling of such sacred ministries. In the days to come, many other gifts were given through the laying on of hands and prophecy—but only after much prayer and fasting. They knew they could not afford to be laying hands on people carelessly. The Lord must indicate *who* was ready to receive such ministry.

Even when the prophetic word was given, still they would double-check its validity, and they would go to their knees to see it these things were really so. They also learned the importance of judging one another's prophecies according to the instruction in I Corinthians 14:29. Every prophecy was evaluated immediately, and no one was offended at having his prophecy thus examined. In fact, they all seemed eager to have their prophecies checked out, and they would ask one another, "Was I on the beam? Was that of God, or did you feel there was a shade of human element in it?" And it was this humble, open-minded approach to this ministry which opened the floodgates of Heaven for the great outpouring of the Holy Spirit that was to follow.

But still the problem of how to regulate the use of this ministry was not fully solved. It seemed quite apparent to everyone at the Bible school that the scriptural instances they'd found of gifts being imparted through prophecy and the laying on of hands were done by seasoned, mature Christians. And even though everyone at the school was trying to be very cautious and reverent in their approach to this ministry, still they all realized what a Pandora's box this could turn out to be if it fell into the hands of the wrong people. They knew there had to be a better answer on how to keep a checkrein on the possible abuse of such a beautiful manifestation of the Spirit.

As I stood there listening to Al Handlin's story about Jon, I could see the dangers involved. I remembered Paul's warning about allowing novices to have too much leadership in the Church. It would certainly be a sad thing for the gifts of the Spirit to become the playthings of the spiritually immature.

"But then," Al went on, "you came along today with your teaching from the Word of God about local church membership, and how every minister should belong to a local church and be under the discipline of that church. And you know," he said, "*that's* the answer to

147

our whole problem! The kind of New Testament Church order you have described would provide the necessary protection against wildfire and excesses that might creep in through those who do not fully understand the leading of the Holy Spirit. If the government of each local church were in the hands of a proved, mature ministry, with mature deacons and elders, then they could correct any problems that might arise."

It made a lot of sense.

Isrealson and I traveled back to Edmonton the next day a great deal wiser. I had learned something about the ministry of laying on of hands, and little by little I began to be open to the leadings of the Spirit on this matter. But because it was new to most of us, I wanted to be very cautious about it, just as the brethren in Saskatchewan had been.

Often we fasted as many as ten days before we laid hands on anyone. We wanted to avoid ministering on the merely human level. We wanted to be wholly given over to the Holy Spirit, so that any ministry which was manifested would be by direct illumination and revelation of the Holy Spirit. We wanted no errors in this ministry of laying our hands on folks and prophesying over them. There must be no reproach brought upon the Lord's work.

As the Lord opened up this ministry to me, I often stood in awe at its beauty and simplicity. It made a tremendous impact on our church, especially when a gift was given which began functioning immediately. We were soon hearing reports that this same spiritual phenomenon was being manifested all across Canada and down through the States. Stella and I rejoiced as we saw how God was restoring His power to the Church.

It soon became evident, however, that the concern of the brethren in Saskatchewan was not without foundation. A number of young brethren who had more zeal than wisdom started laying hands on anybody and everybody and prophesying over them. At first it created a great stir; but when their prophecies did not materialize, much disrepute was brought upon the work of God, and things that were of fanatical proportions crept in and became a hindrance to the real moving of the Spirit. I was not surprised at this, though, for I knew that every move of the Holy Spirit is followed by a countermove of the enemy.

I remembered how Moses had turned his rod into a serpent as a sign to rebellious Pharoah. Immediately the magicians of Egypt were called in, and they duplicated the miracle. The outward mechanics of the two miracles were the same; but the first miracle was produced by the power of God, while the second was produced by satanic power. I knew also the warning in I Timothy 4:1 that "in the latter times some shall depart from the faith, giving heed to seducing spirits, and doctrines of devils."

So I knew the devil was using these novices and their counterfeit prophecies to counteract the true working of the Holy Spirit, thus causing some honest men in the churches to look with disfavor upon what God was doing. But I remembered how this ministry had been launched with such caution and sincerity. I remembered also the tremendous impact of this ministry when it was operating in the power of the Spirit. I talked it over with Stella, and we came to an agreement. We could not surrender a Bible truth simply because the devil was kicking dust into people's eyes and causing confusion on the subject. We knew God would come out on top in the end. (I remembered how Moses' serpent swallowed up all the serpents of the magicians!) We made up our minds to be true to the Word of God, even if it meant misunderstanding.

"Lord," I said, "I don't know what my brother ministers are going to do about this. I don't know what stand they'll take. But as for me, I cannot deny Your power which I have seen manifested through the laying on of hands and prophecy. I know this is real; I know it is genuine; even if *all* of my brethren reject it, still I must accept it. I will continue on in this ministry at any cost!"

I was happy to discover some time later that many of the brethren in a number of the churches in our fellowship were still open to this ministry. And little by little, more and more churches came to have a clearer understanding of this phase of God's work. So I knew that God was working.

Finally, we formed a fellowship of churches known as the *Independent Assemblies of God International*. Many churches became a part of our fellowship, believing that we ought to work and pray together for an outpouring of the Holy spirit. I felt sure that something unusual was about to happen.

CHAPTER THIRTEEN

The Falling of the Mantle

"*Thus saith the Lord,*" the man declared, "*I will now pour out My Spirit upon all denominations . . . .*"

It was the year 1948. I was sitting in a large church in Saskatchewan, Canada, where many people were gathered for an interdenominational Full Gospel convention. They had come from all over Canada and the States to be there; the presence of God had been manifest. It was during an afternoon service that a man suddenly stood to his feet and began to speak to that vast congregation in measured, almost poetic, prophecy:

"*Thus saith the Lord—this is the day that I am moving afresh by My Spirit—I will pour out My Spirit upon the Catholic Church—and upon the priests and bishops*

152

. . . . *They shall prophesy—they shall speak in other tongues—they shall be baptized in My Holy Spirit.*"

In 1948 nothing seemed more unlikely. The whole Church picture was rather gloomy. Many congregations were suffering post-war declines in attendance. The Church seemed hopelessly divided into Protestant, Catholic, fundamentalist and liberal camps, and none of these groups seemed much interested in the others. It was a time of spiritual dryness. Any prospect of an outpouring of the Spirit seemed highly unlikely. But the man went on:

"*I will pour out My Spirit upon the Lutherans—upon the Methodists—upon the Presbyterians—upon the Baptists—upon the Episcopalians!*"

"God," I said, "can that be possible?" I doubt if there was anyone in that place who knew of a single Spirit-filled Catholic priest. None of us had ever heard a nun speak in tongues. And whoever heard of a Spirit-filled Presbyterian? Or a Spirit-filled Episcopalian? In fact, if there was *one* thing about which all the divided groups of Christendom agreed, it was that they wanted nothing to do with "those crazy Pentecostals."

So no wonder I smiled at that prophecy. (I suspect there were a good many other smiles of disbelief in that congregation.) None of us dared to dream that by the year 1972, there would be thousands upon thousands of Spirit-filled Christians in both Catholic and Protestant churches!

There was no denying the fact that something unusual had been happening in the last few years, even in my own ministry. I often had the strange feeling that God was getting ready to do something new.

"Could this be it?" I wondered. "Could it be possible that God is getting ready to fulfill the ancient prophecy about the latter day outpouring of the Holy Spirit?" I wanted to believe it, but it seemed so unlikely . . . .

Not long after that, God spoke to me even more plainly. I was guest speaker at a convention in Canada. After a refreshing night's sleep I woke up early, invigorated and ready to start the day. But first of all, there was a yearning in my soul to pray and seek the face of the Lord. While I was praying, a peculiar vision came to me.

I saw a vast harvest field of grain, as far as the eye could see to the north, to the south, and to the west. I saw the wind moving over the grain, spreading out into long ripples like the rolling waves of the sea. The overripe heads of grain bobbed and bowed before the wind, begging to be harvested.

Then as I looked out beyond the horizon, I saw massive cumulus clouds beginning to come together, until there was a solid front of clouds that rose high and black. I saw distant lightning beginning to flash across those clouds. I heard thunder rolling in the distance. The air became yellowish and murky.

Having been raised on a midwestern farm, I realized what the approaching storm could do to a field of ripe wheat. Where there had been a bountiful harvest waiting to be reaped, a ruined crop would lie on the ground, beaten down by slashing rain and pellets of ice. I had seen our neighbors, as well as our own family, hasten to the harvest field when such a storm was threatening, and attempt to gather in as much grain as possible before it was too late.

While these scenes passed before my mind, I became aware that what I was seeing had some spiritual significance, and that God was trying to tell me something. "Lord," I asked, "what does it mean?"

I soon began to get understanding. The field represented the world. The moving wind was the Holy Spirit. Each stalk of grain was a soul ready to be gathered into the Kingdom of God. The clouds represented the last chapter of this age, preceding the return of Jesus. The thunder and lightning were warnings of the shortness of time.

Then something else began to happen. I saw the reapers running out into the fields, sickles in hand. They began to hack away, gathering in the sheaves as quickly as they could.

"Hurry!" they shouted to one another in desperation. "The storm is coming!"

But they knew it was no use. It would take some kind of superhuman power to get the job done in time. They were doing the best they could, but it wasn't enough.

Then I noticed something coming down through the clouds. At first, I couldn't make out what it was. But as it floated down toward the earth, whipping and flapping in the wind, I recognized it as a mantle. Down, down it came, majestically. For a moment it hovered over the great harvest field, and then suddenly parted into many portions which settled down upon the reapers. Instantly, a marvelous change came over them. They began to reap with such speed and agility that I was amazed. Even the expression on their faces changed. Instead of gloom and despair at the prospect of a lost harvest, they began to radiate faith and confidence.

"We can do it now," they called to one another joyfully. "We've got the power!"

They didn't even seem to get tired. On and on they worked. Not a drop of rain fell. It was as though the storm was holding its fury until the harvest was gathered in. The mantle had made the difference.

The significance of the mantle was very clear to me. I had often read the story of the

156

old prophet Elijah, and how his successor Elisha had asked for a double portion of the Spirit that was upon Elijah. I remembered, too, how that desire was granted when the mantle of Elijah became his. The mantle was a symbol of the power of the Holy Spirit. Elisha knew that without special power, he could not do the work to which he had been called. But with the mantle, all things were possible.

It was then that the meaning of the vision became crystal-clear. "This is the age of the last great harvest," I said to myself. "There are so many people to be brought to Christ, and His coming is so near that much of the harvest will be lost unless the Holy Spirit gives us special power." I knew that better tools were not the answer. "We need the mantle," I said under my breath. "If the apostles needed the power of the Holy Spirit in their day, then we need a *double portion* of that same Spirit. And we need it now!"

A short time later, I was to speak at a week-long camp meeting in Plainfield, Vermont. There was a warm glow of the Spirit that seemed to follow along with me as I crossed the Canadian border into the States. I knew it was going to be a very special camp meeting.

The services were held in a tabernacle which would seat around four hundred people. The first thing that arrested my attention about those services was the prophetic messages being given by the people. They were saying identically the same things I had heard in Canada: that God was getting ready to pour out His Spirit and that all denominations would be included in this outpouring.

"This is God," I said to myself. "These people have not talked to the Canadian brethren; they've not communicated in any way. And yet, here they are speaking the same thing. Certainly, this is not man's doing—this is God operating through the Holy Spirit."

I had been staying at a motel in the village. One morning as I came out to the campgrounds, a group of excited brethren met me and all began to talk at once,

"Brother Rasmussen!" one said. "Guess what happened last night!"

Without waiting for a reply, another took up the story.

"We had just settled down in our tent for the night, and everything was just getting quiet, when suddenly all of us felt the strangest vibration coming over us."

"We didn't know *what* it was," another put in.

The first speaker continued: "So all of us got up and went outside, and there, up in the night sky, was the strangest thing we've ever

seen. There were beams of light coming down
from heaven from many different directions.
There was also a banner of light which seemed
to be directly over the tabernacle. It was
gently waving, like a banner in the breeze.
While we stood there watching all this, those
shafts of light from heaven kept coming down
and down, until finally they converged on the
ampitheater over there among those cedar
trees. We all felt the power of God come
down over us, and we started to sway gently
back and forth, as though blown by an unfelt
wind."

I questioned them carefully. All of them
agreed about what they had seen. All of them
insisted that they had seen this sight literally,
with their own eyes. None of them were puzzled by what they had seen. They were convinced that they had seen a manifestation of
the glory of God, and that God's Spirit would
be mightily poured out upon us that day.
They were overflowing with praise and
thanksgiving. Before that day was over, I was
to be fully convinced of the reality of what
they had seen.

We met in the tabernacle at 8 o'clock. The
meeting was opened with prayer, and I sensed
a tremendous uplift of the Spirit. When the
time came for the ministry of the Word, I be-

gan to teach them about the ministry of laying on of hands. I showed them that this is one of the fundamental doctrines of the Bible, that it is named in Hebrew 6:1, 2 as being one of the *principles* of the doctrine of Christ, and one of the *foundational* things. I went on to show them how the various gifts of the Holy Spirit may function through the laying on of hands: how the sick can be healed; how blessings can be bestowed; how prophecies can be spoken; how the knowledge and wisdom of God can be imparted; how the gifts of the Spirit can be released in an individual: all through the laying on of hands.

After I had taught them thoroughly, then I began to lay my hands on the people. And, oh, the power that was unleashed in that meeting! Some were receiving miraculous healings, while others were praying for salvation, and still others were receiving the baptism in the Spirit. I marveled at how so many things could be going on at once, and yet be so orderly!

When the lunch bell rang, nobody was interested in going to lunch. They rang that old bell again and again. Finally a handful sifted out to eat, but the majority stayed right there in the tabernacle.

Then I saw Pastor Gustaf Berglund coming from the back of the tabernacle with a teenaged girl who seemed to be hopelessly crippled. She was wearing a steel brace on one leg.

160

My heart went out to her in compassion, and oh, how I wanted to help her! But the sight of the ugly brace caused me to falter for a moment.

"Who does Brother Berglund think I am?" I asked myself. "After all, this is going to take a *miracle!*"

And then I remember that I sensed within me the sweet voice of Jesus. He neither chided nor condemned me for my unbelief. It was just a simple question.

"*Who is going to do this?*" He asked. "*You or Me?*"

"Jesus," I responded, "*You're* going to do it." I was immediately relieved. I saw that my only responsibility was to lay my hands on the young lady. The Spirit of Jesus was within me. My hands were *His*, and I knew He wanted to lay *His* hands on her. The power that surged through my hands was *His* power, and the miracle would be *His* miracle.

So, very simply, I laid my hands on Janie's head and began to pray for her.

"Dear God," I said, "I pray in the name of Jesus that you will grant a miracle to this young lady. I ask that this infirmity may leave, and that perfect life and health may come back into her lifeless limb."

That was all. I had done what Jesus wanted me to do. The rest would be up to Him. I didn't feel like asking her to remove the brace, although that would have been very spectacular. But, for the moment, it seemed that I should just let her go on her way, and commit the whole thing to Jesus. As Janie thump-thumped back to her seat, all of us were deeply moved with compassion for her. By all outward appearances, nothing had happened. But I was confident that the miracle would appear in due time.

That meeting went on and on all afternoon. When Mrs. Jacobsen from Brooklyn, New York, came forward for prayer, she explained to me that she was afflicted with a skin disease which she had had for many years. All kinds of medication had been tried. Many doctors had prescribed various kinds of treatments. I could see how her skin was still scaling and peeling. Nothing had helped.

When I laid my hands on her, immediately the power of God came down upon her. She threw up her hands and began to dance and praise God. Overly emotional, you say? Well, I was tempted to think so for a moment too— until I caught a glimpse of her arms. Her skin was as perfect as the skin of a baby.

The supper bell rang. A few went to eat, but most of them were too caught up in the Spirit to be concerned about food. So they stayed on, and the meeting went on until late that night. Miracle after miracle took place. When we gave the invitation for those who wanted to know Jesus, scores of people came to the front of that tabernacle. It was a time of great rejoicing as many opened up to Jesus, and others were baptized in the Spirit.

I finally got to bed that night around one o'clock. As I pillowed my head and looked up into the face of God, I was one tired but happy man. I thought about all that had happened during that eventful day. Then I remembered what that excited group of men had seen the night before. Shafts of light! Banner of glory! There was no better way to describe what we had experienced that day. I thought and thought about that, and finally drifted off to sleep . . . .

The next morning I was up early and back out to the campgrounds in time for breakfast. In fact, I was a few minutes early, so I sat down on a bench beside the tabernacle, waiting for the breakfast bell to ring. As I was sitting there, a young girl came skipping down from the ladies' dormitory. It was Janie, the lame girl I had prayed for the day before!

"Guess what's happened!" she said, coming up to me with a bounce.

I didn't need to guess. It was perfectly obvious what had happened.

"In the middle of the night," she said breathlessly, "I felt something going through my legs. It was like a thousand needles beginning to prick my body where I had no feeling.

It went down through my ankles. Oh, it was so wonderful!"

"Do you know what that prickly sensation was?" I asked. "It was life coming into your foot again. The power of God has brought your foot back to life."

We both rejoiced and praised the Lord.

"Janie," I said, "tell me how you came to be in this condition."

She told me that four years before, she had been out on her uncle's farm at hay-mowing time. He had been trying hard to get the job done, so her aunt had packed a lunch for her husband and asked Janie to take it out to him. Rather than walk all the way, Janie decided to get the horse out of the barn and ride out.

It was a lot of fun trotting out through the fields. The smell of fresh-mown hay filled the air, and she could hear the steady clatter-clatter of the mowing machine. In a few minutes, she was there, and was preparing to dismount, when the horse, apparently frightened at the mower, reared and threw Janie off onto the ground, right into the path of the mowing machine. Her uncle saw it and tried to stop, but it was too late. Bringing his tractor to a squeaky halt, he looked down at her, horrified. Her foot had been cut off at the ankle, and was just dangling by the skin.

She was rushed to the hospital. Hoping against hope, the doctors performed emergency surgery, and sewed the foot to the ankle. In a few weeks, to everyone's amazement, the doctors reported that it had been a success and the foot was growing back on. But there was no feeling. The nerves had been hopelessly severed, and nothing could be done. So she had to be fitted with a brace, and she would have to put up with her "dead foot" for the rest of her life.

"But now look at me!" she exclaimed. "I've got a new ankle!" She twisted her foot in every direction, and it moved just as freely and naturally as her other foot. There was no difference at all.

"You know," she said, "the only part of my foot where I don't have feeling is my little toe."

"Maybe God is going to leave that," I replied. "Perhaps God wants you to have a reminder of your affliction, so that you'll never forget how He worked a miracle for you."

On Monday morning, I started back to Canada. There was plenty of time during that 2,000-mile trip to meditate and pray. As my mind went back over all the amazing experiences of the past week, it came to me that we had seen a manifestation of almost every gift of the Holy Spirit mentioned in First Corinthians 12.

"Praise the Lord!" I said aloud. "God *is* restoring His power to the Church." But I knew it was just the beginning.

Back in Canada, we continued to witness the increasing manifestations of the Spirit in our church and Bible school. We also continued to hear reports of revival spreading from state to state, province to province, and nation to nation. I began to have a great yearning to be traveling from place to place so that I might be a part of what God was doing. As often as I could, I accepted speaking engagements in other parts of Canada and the States. Finally I received an invitation to have a special series of services at the Philadelphia Church in Chicago—the church I had previously served as pastor. The letter stated that the people had heard of the moving of God's Spirit, and that both the people and the pastor were desirous of knowing more about what God was doing.

"I think you ought to go," Stella said. "I'll stay here and pray for you." So off I went to Chicago.

I'll never forget the Wednesday night meeting. I was preaching from the fifteenth chapter of John.

"I am the true vine," I read, "and my Father is the husbandman. Every branch in me that beareth not fruit he taketh away."

It was a familiar passage. Probably most of

166

the congregation could have quoted it from memory.

"And every branch that beareth fruit," I continued, "he [the Father] purgeth it, that it may bring forth more fruit. Now ye are clean through the word which I have spoken unto you. Abide in me, and I in you. As the branch cannot bear fruit of itself, except it abide in the vine; no more can ye, except ye abide in me. I am the vine, ye are the branches: He that abideth in me, and I in him, the same bringeth forth much fruit: for without me ye can do nothing."

As I read to them, I sensed the Holy Spirit coming upon me with great illumination of the Word. I explained to them, in simple language, the absolute necessity of abiding in the Jesus-vine. This is the secret of producing the fruit and the gifts of the Spirit. I showed them that the same life which is in the vine must flow into the branches. It is Jesus' life and power *in us* which make the Spirit-filled life possible.

"The world will never know that Jesus is real," I declared, "until they see His power in us, confirming the Word of God with signs following! These signs are the gifts of the Holy Spirit. They are done supernaturally. God, through His Spirit, is able to illumine our minds, give us wisdom, give us knowledge, give us power to glorify God—and when the world sees these signs, they will acknowledge as they did in the days of Jesus, 'No man can do these miracles that thou doest, except God be with him.' "

The spiritual hunger of those people just seemed to *pull* the preaching out of me. What a tremendous service we had! It was good to be back in Chicago and see God working in such a mighty way.

The next morning, I awoke just as dawn was breaking. (The church sexton and his wife had graciously offered to let me stay in their spare bedroom.) I stretched, and cracked my eyelids open just enough to see the light of day beginning to penetrate a little parting in the draperies. Just as I was thinking that I should get up, I felt a hand on my right shoulder.

A series of quick thoughts flashed through my mind.

"Who *is* that? I'm sure the door didn't open. I didn't hear anyone coming in . . . ."

For a split second, I hesitated to open my eyes. There was something about the feeling of that hand that made me very uneasy. It seemed as though there was someone in the room who was not in harmony with me.

"What is this?" I wondered. I had had such a sweet anointing the night before in preaching the Word, and such a good night's rest. I couldn't understand what this was that I was sensing now. As I turned to look, there

I saw the devil standing by the bed with his hand on my shoulder.

I knew he was there to stop me. He knew I was about to be launched into the greatest phase of my ministry.

"Satan," I said firmly, "I command you to get out of here in the name of Jesus! I command you to go!"

I had no sooner said that than my eyes were open to the things of the Spirit, and I saw the angel of the Lord in my room. This angel took Satan by the shoulders, and with a swish, he was out of the room. The unpleasant feeling suddenly vanished. Needless to say, by that time I was wide awake!

I looked toward the window; the light was even brighter now than it was before. *As I gazed at that light streaming in over the foot of my bed, my eyes were opened again, and I saw Jesus standing before me.*

I reveled in the beauty of His blazing glory. I saw His penetrating eyes, His hands folded across His waist, the luminous white garment draped down from His shoulders. I lay there in amazement, waiting for Him to speak. But He didn't say a word. Instead, it was as though His thoughts came into my mind.

"My son," He said, "I am watching over you."

And then He vanished . . . .

There was a warm glow in my soul as I got

169

up that morning. Something great was about to happen.

"What will it be?" I wondered. "Has the time come for the Spirit to be poured out on all denominations? Is Jesus getting ready to come back?" And then, as an afterthought, I asked, "Lord, is this the beginning of the last chapter?"

I pulled back the drapes, looked up into a beautiful blue sky, and smiled at the Holy Spirit.

CHAPTER FOURTEEN

You Can't Hurry God

I had learned that when God shuts and bolts a door, you must not try to get in through the window. But I was also to learn that God sometimes unbolts doors that He has previously shut.

In 1950, I received an invitation to return to my old Philadelphia Church in Chicago to be their pastor again. Believing this to be God's will, I accepted the invitation, and began to enjoy the second time around with those precious people. It was a real joy, but I was sure it wouldn't be for long.

During those days, I was invited to be one of the speakers at Camp Byron over in Wisconsin. In one of the evening services, there was a great manifestation of the Holy Spirit through the laying on of hands. Some of the people wanted to lay hands on me.

"Fine!" I said. "I always appreciate the prayers of God's people."

While they were praying, one of the women began to prophesy. "My!" she said, stepping back two or three steps. "What I see!" And she began to tell of a worldwide ministry which God had in store for me. As she spoke, the presence of God came down over me, and I knew she was speaking by revelation. I saw in a flash that my mission was much larger than Tacoma or Chicago or Brooklyn. My mind went back to what I had said to the Lord years before in The Light of the World Mission—"I'll go wherever God wants me to go —If He wants me to go to Africa—I'm willing to go . . . ." I went back to Chicago, sure that my next move would be overseas.

But still God kept me waiting.

Imagine my surprise 2 years later when I went to the mailbox and found an invitation to return to Tacoma, Washington, and again become the pastor of the Bethel Pentecostal Assembly!

"Again, Lord?" I asked in amazement. "I'm already doing a second round here in Chicago. Why should I do the same thing in Tacoma?" I wanted to dismiss the idea. Why go to Tacoma when there was Africa, and the islands of the sea, and . . . .

But God stopped me.

"The time is not yet," He seemed to say. *"You are to go to Tacoma. This is My doing. Go, and do not doubt."*

So, in 1952 we packed up our belongings and our five boys (we had gained Paul) and moved to Tacoma. It was like a second honeymoon. Old friendships were renewed. New contacts were made. It was a happy time of growth, and it didn't take me long to recapture that old comfortable feeling I had had in the same church almost twenty years before.

The weeks rolled up into months, the months into years. Every now and then I thought about the prophecy at Camp Byron, and wondered when God was going to move me overseas. Or would He ever? I knew the prophecy had been given in utmost sincerity. Still, there was the possibility of a mistake. Then, one day I looked at the calendar and was startled to realize that I had now been in Tacoma for ten years!

"Lord," I prayed, "there must be some mistake. Surely ten years is enough time for You to keep Your promise to me!" But then I was reminded that God doesn't reckon time as we do. So I waited a little longer. Finally, in 1963, an unexpected letter arrived.

It was from our good friend, Pastor Joseph

Mattsson-Boze, who was laboring in East Africa. He was inviting me, along with some others, to join him in Kenya for a seminar for native student-pastors. Both Stella and I felt the time had now come for a new chapter in our lives, so I wrote back to Pastor Mattsson-Boze, and told him I would come.

Kenya wasn't exactly the easiest place to begin. I had learned that the Gospel had been preached there for hundreds of years, and yet there had been a steady decline in conversions, and the Church had fallen into lethargy and formalism. In fact, there were very few born-again Christians to be found in the churches, and to all appearances Christianity was dying a slow death in that country. But I knew that the same God who had been pouring out His Spirit in so many places could also work in Kenya. The mere fact that there was interest in such a seminar was encouraging. I was even more encouraged when I arrived in Nairobi and found 120 African students who could hardly wait for the meetings to begin.

Our team of workers gave them eight solid hours of Bible study every day, going steadily from 8 in the morning until noon, taking an hour's break for lunch, and then going on again until 5. I'll never forget those boys.

174

They were like sponges. They soaked up everything we could give them and still thirsted for more. The radiance of their faces as they listened to the Word of God was indeed heart warming.

We taught them how to become ministers of true New Testament churches. We explained the plan of God for the Church today, and showed them that the power of the Spirit is necessary for success in Christian witnessing. We showed them out of the Scriptures that it is God's will for their churches to be strong, self-governing, self-supporting units within the framework of the Lord's Body. We taught them about the gifts of the Spirit and showed them how they could go out and minister in the power of the Spirit, healing the sick, casting out devils, just as Jesus did. The more we taught them, the more their joy increased, and they would break out into singing in their Kiswahili tongue.

It wasn't long until we began to see results. One day one of the missionaries said to me, "Let's go out and visit a church that one of our national pastors has pioneered."

"Oh, I'd be glad to!" I said, for I had heard that already some of the student pastors were seeing results in their churches.

I'll never forget what I saw as we approached that little mud-hut village. The pastor was a very little man, but he was full of zeal and fire. He had accompanied us out to

175

the village, and as we were walking through that village, I was astonished to see the natives bow low before us, saying something in Kiswahili.

"Do you know what they're saying?" one of the missionaries asked me.

"No, what?"

"They're saying, 'Here come the gods! Here come the gods!' "

Well, we soon straightened them out about that. But as I thought it out afterwards, I realized that they had said this because of the tremendous power which had been manifested through their pastor's ministry. He had been in the training seminars and then had gone out and taught his people, and had been doing exactly what Jesus said he should do. I remembered how the people of Lystra had said the same thing about Paul and Barnabas in Acts 14, when they healed a cripple. There too, the crowds had been impressed by the power of God working in men, and had simply assumed that these men were gods. When I learned that this little pastor had been laying hands on the sick, healing all kinds of diseases, casting out demons by the Word and Spirit of God, and even raising the dead, then I understood why the natives thought we were supernatural beings. I rejoiced to see what an impact had been made on these people by the preaching of the Gospel through this little national pastor.

You should have seen him beam with holy pride when he showed us the church they had built out of sticks and mud. In our eyes it wasn't any masterpiece of architecture, but they had done the very best they could. I knew God must have a very tender love for those simple people who crowded around their church, chattering happily. It was as holy as any elaborate temple I had ever seen, and it afforded them the protection they needed from the hot sun and the rain. That was all that mattered.

When we stepped inside, I found the whole building packed with people who had come to hear the Gospel. Other people on the outside were looking through the open windows, trying to see and hear what was going on inside. In fact, there were more people on the outside than there were within.

"You know," the little pastor whispered to me, "we began this congregation under a tree just a year ago. Now we have this church and hundreds of people." I put my arm around him and rejoiced with tears in my eyes and a lump in my throat.

The service was power-filled. When the invitation was given, so many came forward that we hardly knew what to do with them. After the service was over, the pastor, along with some of his elders, went down to a little water hole not far from the church and baptized eighty converts. It was a beautiful sight to behold. I felt a warm glow in my soul when we came to the end of that day. How I enjoyed writing to Stella that night and telling her all about the wonderful things God had done!

The seminar sessions moved on with great success. I knew these young students were the hope of the Church in Kenya. But, oh, how they needed the power of the Holy Spirit! One evening, when we were all assembled in the city park where we were having our meetings, I asked them a question.

"How many of you have not yet received the baptism in the Holy Spirit?"

Fifty-nine hands were lifted.

I felt the time had come for me to do some very plain teaching on this subject. So I opened my Bible and began to show them how much they needed this deeper relationship with Jesus.

"The Bible says, 'Ye shall receive power, after that the Holy Ghost is come upon you: and ye shall be witnesses unto me,'" I quoted from Acts 1:8. "Now we have come to teach you to witness, but no one can witness effectively without the power of the Holy Spirit."

I talked about many other scriptures, and they never missed a single word. It was so quiet, even the birds in the trees seemed to be listening.

"Please understand," I went on, "that the baptism in the Spirit is not a reward; it is a gift from God. Anyone who is washed in the blood of Jesus is a candidate for this experience. Through the Holy Spirit, you can have power to witness and power to live a holy and victorious Christian life. You can be a testimony to the Church and to the world at large."

I knew the moment had come when the Spirit would be poured out on many of those young students. My fingers tingled with the power of God.

"If you desire to be baptized in the Spirit right now," I said, "come and let me lay my hands upon you in the name of Jesus. You can receive the power of the Spirit just as they did in Samaria when Peter and John laid hands on them, and just as they did in Ephesus."

After I had instructed them simply and clearly, fifty-nine of them came forward for prayer. I laid my hands on them one by one, and prayed for each one individually. One by one, they received the Spirit, and began to speak in tongues. By the time I was finished praying, all those student pastors were praising God at once, and worshipping in tongues, just as the 120 did on the day of Pentecost. What a glorious scene that was!

Suddenly I remembered the Mayor!

Since we were holding our services in the city park, the Mayor had given us an order that we were to close the meetings at 9 o'clock, so that no one in the neighborhood would be disturbed. I glanced at my watch, and sure enough, it was past nine. I could just see us all being arrested for disturbing the peace!

I jumped up on a table we had there and began to clap my hands, hoping to get their attention.

"Stop! Stop! Stop!" I shouted at the top of my voice, adding even more noise to the holy uproar. But they were so carried away in the Spirit, they had not the slightest notion of stopping. And I don't think a one of them heard me.

Finally, I said to Frederick, my interpreter, "You'll have to go through this crowd and make them get quiet. Hurry!"

So he quickly moved out through that crowd, telling them to be quiet. Little by little, the praising and shouting subsided, and they turned and looked at me as though I had just quenched the Holy Spirit.

"I know how happy you are," I explained, "but I forgot to tell you that the Mayor has asked us to have our meetings closed by 9 o'clock. We must not disturb the neighbors, for as you know, many are in bed right now, and we must not bring any reproach on our Lord."

They agreed and seemed to understand perfectly.

"I don't want you to quench the Holy Spirit, though," I continued, "so just go on your way rejoicing, speaking quietly in tongues, and glorifying God. It's all right; the Lord appreciates quiet praises just as much as loud ones."

Then, just before dismissing them, I said, "Tell me, how many of you have received the baptism in the Spirit?" All fifty-nine hands went up.

A few days later, when our plane took off for America, I looked down on the city and villages below with thanksgiving. Somehow, I knew this was just the beginning . . . .

CHAPTER FIFTEEN

Our Plans are not His Plans

Tacoma was never quite the same to me after that. From that time on, the only country I could ever call home was the one which most needed the Gospel.

I began to make plans for other trips. Stella wanted to travel with me ever so badly, but she hadn't been feeling well for some reason. We prayed together about the matter, but no answer came.

In 1964, I received an invitation from Borge and Doris Langerud to come to Jamaica. Borge and Doris were friends of ours who had gone to that island some years before to carry the message of the outpouring of God's Spirit, and to build New Testament churches. After a few days of prayer, God again made it clear to Stella and me that it was His will for me to accept the invitation. The people of the church in Tacoma rejoiced along with me at these opportunities to take the Gospel overseas. They too were beginning to see that God was opening new doors of service for me, and I think they knew I wouldn't be with them much longer.

When I arrived in Jamaica, my spirit was again overwhelmed with the same joy I had felt in Kenya. People were hungry for the Gospel message. Everywhere I went the crowds came, and I sensed a great anointing of the Spirit upon me as I preached the message of Jesus. There were many conversions, and many were baptized in the Spirit. Borge and Doris had done a good job of preparing the way before me, and I spoke at a number of conventions and visited many churches. Everywhere I went, people rejoiced to hear of the outpouring of God's Spirit throughout the world.

One night, after a busy day of preaching, I began to think about Stella again. How good God had been to give me a companion who was so full of compassion and consecration to the service of God! Without her help in the office at home, my trips would have been impossible. So often I had been away in conventions, camp meetings and seminars, and she had always been willing to sacrifice my presence and my time. But now that the children had grown, I knew it was an especially

183

lonely time for her. I knew she was longing for the day when she could spend all her time with me in my travels.

"Dear Lord," I said, "you know Stella's not been feeling well lately . . . ."

I was fully confident that God would heal her. Both of us believed in the miracle-working power of God, and we knew it would be easy for Him to clear up this little problem, whatever it was.

"Jesus, lay your healing hand upon her," I pleaded. "You know how much we want to be together."

As I was praying quietly, a vision came before me which left me completely motionless. *I saw exactly what was to happen to her. It was as though God pulled back the veil of time and let me glimpse into the future. I wasn't prepared for what I was to see, but I knew it was from God. I saw that her sickness was far more serious than either of us had guessed. I saw that it would continue to get worse and that there would be no recovery.*

"Do not fear," God said to me. "*I am going to take her home.*"

"But, God . . ." I stammered in confusion.

"*Do not question,*" He said quietly. "*I have shown you My will, that you might not be troubled when it happens. Stella's task is done.*"

"But, Lord, what about Your healing power?"

"When I take her home," He answered, *"she will be healed forever."*

I was stunned into complete silence. I lay there in the dark, tears streaming down my face. It was late in the night when I finally committed it all to Him, and fell asleep in His love.

A few day later, I received a telephone call from the Island of Trinidad. The Superintendent of the Open Bible Standard Church was on the other end of the line, wanting to know if I would accept an invitation to Trinidad to be the commencement speaker at their Bible college, and also speaker for their annual church convention. I hesitated at first. There seemed to be a number of reasons why I shouldn't go. I had a convention scheduled in Peoria, Illinois; I wanted to get home with Stella; and besides I wasn't a member of his denomination. But when I suggested that it might be more fitting to have a speaker from his own denomination, he insisted all the more. Finally, I accepted the invitation, and promised him I would be there at commencement time.

On the way home to Tacoma, I made up my mind that my vision about Stella would remain a secret. She had great faith that God was going to heal her, and I felt that I should do everything possible to encourage her faith, even though God had revealed to me very plainly what He was going to do.

When I saw that she was no better, we both decided that she ought to see the family doctor. So she made an appointment and had a number of tests taken. In a few days, the results of the tests were back, and the doctor asked both of us to come into his office.

"Mrs. Rasmussen," he began, "I have received all of the reports from your tests . . . ."

He paused for a moment as though he hated to go on.

"One of the tests came back positive," he continued. "You have quite an advanced rectal cancer."

I took Stella's hand, hoping to ease the shock. I had expected to hear something of this nature, but Stella was completely unprepared. For a few moments there was silence. Then the doctor continued:

"Of course," he said, "I don't want you to be frightened. We're working with this kind of thing all the time, you know, and there is a possibility that the condition can be corrected through surgery. But you must not wait. Any delay could be very serious."

"Then what chances do I have without surgery?" Stella wanted to know.

"None whatsoever."

She sat there silently, biting her quivering lip. Finally she stood to her feet, drawing herself up to her full height. "Dr. Proud," she said, "you know I never make any decision like this without prayer. Let me have a few days to make up my mind."

"All right," he said, "but only a few days."

The ride back home was strangely silent. I hardly knew what to say. But, once inside the house, we began to talk about what we should do.

"Andrew," she said, "we've always believed in the healing power of the Lord. I don't see why I should go through that operation. I'm convinced that God is able to heal any disease —even cancer!"

We talked it over with the five boys. There were differing opinions, but finally Jon said, "Mother, you've always stood for divine healing and faith in God, and it seems to me that this is the time to prove Him." That settled it for her. There would be no surgery. So she called Dr. Proud and told him about her decision. He deeply regretted her decision and urged her to change her mind. But there was to be no changing.

She began to fast and pray. "Andrew, I know God's going to heal me," she would say. "You just wait and see."

Those were very difficult days for me. I too believed in God's healing power, and yet I knew that "it is appointed unto man once to die." It seemed to me that God had made His appointment with Stella. To be sure, it didn't seem to make any sense in the natural. Stella had been living for the day when she would be free to travel with me, and minister overseas. It was hard to understand why God should deprive her of that which she looked forward to so eagerly. But I knew I couldn't argue with God.

At times, when she was on a fast, she would say to me, "Andrew, why don't *you* fast?" And I did fast some, but not to her satisfaction. She thought I should have gotten desperate with God, and then she would have been healed. It was a difficult position to be in. I knew what God wanted, but I also knew what *we* wanted. So how was I going to pray? If I begged God to let us have our way, would that not be God's second best?

I remembered the story of Hezekiah, and how God had changed His mind and added to his years. "Well," I thought, "if God did that for Hezekiah, He could do that for Stella." So I began to pray along those lines. Many were the hours we prayed together earnestly for God's healing touch. All this time, I kept my secret hidden away in my heart.

Finally the time rolled around for my trip to Peoria and Trinidad. It was difficult to leave Stella, but I felt it was best if I continued to be cheerful and natural, so I put her in

188

God's hands and boarded the big jet for Peoria.

In a few days the convention was over, and I was on my way to Trinidad. I began to think about how good God had been. This would be my third overseas trip. But this one was different since I would not be working with pastors in our own fellowship (Independent Assemblies of God International), but instead I would be ministering to the brethren of the Open Bible Standard Churches. From the beginning I had felt very keenly that our fellowship was not to be a sect, nor a denomination, but rather an interdenominational fellowship which could be a blessing to the whole Body of Christ. So I looked forward to this new experience.

I was warmly welcomed by Open Bible Standard's Superintendent of the West Indies, Rev. William Whitlow. He first took me to the city of San Fernando, where they have their church headquarters for that island. I was introduced to a fine group of missionaries and a great congregation of nationals and workers. They received me with such open arms and with such warmth of fellowship that I felt at home immediately. I knew that I was one of them. That same warmth of the Holy Spirit was present when I spoke to them at the commencement exercises of their Bible school.

One night during the convention that followed, God prompted me to urge the people to bring all of their sick friends to the next meeting. "If they have no way of getting here," I said, "then you bring them. Bring the blind, the halt, the maimed and the demon-possessed. Jesus Christ is the same yesterday, today and forever, and what He did in the days of the apostles, He will do again if you will only believe."

I went on to tell them how they would see the glory of God and how the power of God would be manifested.

The next night there was an awesome scene in that large church auditorium. There were East Indians, Negros and Whites all gathered together in the unity of the Holy Spirit. God came down upon me in great power as I preached the Gospel, and afterwards I prayed for the sick. One after another received miraculous healings, until it seemed that there was hardly a sick person left in that auditorium.

After the service, Rev. Whitlow said to me, "Brother Rasmussen, all my life I have been wanting to see something like this; but I didn't know whether I would see it or not. But in these meetings I'm seeing it. Everyone you prayed for tonight was healed."

It went on that way night after night. At times I thought it strange that all those people should be healed, but not Stella. But then I remembered that God had clearly revealed His will about her. So I went on in those meetings, and great miracles took place every night.

I remember one particular Wednesday. We were having an afternoon service that day, and the large church auditorium was quickly filling up. Among those coming in were three women who caught my attention. Two of them were quite large, happy, Negro women, and between them was a very small East Indian woman looking like an unhappy thorn between two uncommonly large roses. Holding onto her arms, they brought her in and sat her down right on the front seat.

It wasn't long until I knew what her problem was. As I preached under the power of the Holy Spirit, she became greatly agitated and refused to sit still. She would leave her seat, run out the side door, and these two dear Negro women would follow her out. They would then take her by the arms, bring her back in, sit her down in her seat and hold her there. I recognized immediately that the woman was being troubled by demons.

She would sit still as long as the other two women were holding her. But sometimes they would get so taken up in the service that they would forget themselves and let go of her. Up she'd be again, and out the door, and these two dear sisters would go after her and bring her back. This happened again and again during the meeting, but I refused to let it bother me.

Sometimes this little woman would challenge me as I was preaching, and the demons would speak out through her to disturb me and ruin the meeting. The more she interfered, the louder I preached. I was determined not to give any undue attention to these demons during the service. I had a message to preach, and I thanked God that He had given me a built-in amplifier. So I boomed out my message and completely drowned her out.

At the close of the meeting, I invited the unsaved to accept Jesus, and we had a great time of prayer together. Then we prayed for the sick, and many were healed. Finally, I went over to this little East Indian woman and looked her right in the face. I felt the love of Jesus rising up within me, urging me to do something for this poor woman.

"You devils," I said as I looked at her, "you spirits from the pit of hell, how many of you are in there?"

"What are you going to do to us?" they screamed back at me. "What are you going to do to us?"

I had carefully studied how Jesus dealt with demon spirits, and was not surprised at their reactions and their fear of me. So I proceeded with the authority which I knew was mine in Christ.

"I will tell you what I am going to do with you after you tell me your names," I said, "and after you know who *I* am."

I then proceeded to overcome them by the word of my testimony: "I am a son of the living God," I declared. "I believe in Jesus! His blood covers all my sins! He has saved me and given me eternal life!"

They didn't like my mention of Jesus' name, and the woman began to struggle to get free from the two women who were holding her. But I went right on.

"Jesus has given me *power* over all of you evil spirits," I said. "You are going to obey me as I speak to you in His name. Give me your names, and tell me how many of you are in there!"

At that, a strange voice spoke through the little woman's lips and said, "There are ten of us." They began to scream out their names, and one of the missionaries who was especially interested jotted their names down on a slip of paper as they were given. I stood firm on the authority of Jesus as each demon cried out his name.

"Shoal!"

"Hemraj!"

"Thageeran!"

"A dumb spirit!"

"Hermonath Sadhoo!"

"Daly, killer of children!"

"Rookminia, a religious spirit from India!"

"Gibbon!"

"George, an unclean spirit!"

"Doon Doon!"

193

One of the missionaries recognized the last name. A teen-aged girl by that name who lived in the same house with this East Indian woman had committed suicide only a short time before. We concluded that the name "Doon Doon" indicated the presence of a suicidal demon.

I then proceeded to name them one by one, binding them in the name of Jesus, and casting them out. The one named George was especially noisy.

"I come from America," he said loudly. "I come from Georgia! I am an unclean spirit!" Then he laughed, mocked and ridiculed.

"Hold your peace," I commanded. "Come out of that woman right now. In the name of Jesus, obey me."

Instantly the noisy laughing stopped and I knew she had been saved from "unclean George."

As I looked at her, I realized how important it is for Christians to be compassionate toward people who are bound by demons. Sometimes we show great disgust and distaste for people who are bound by cruelty, filthy habits and lust. But we need to remember that many of these people have been brought to the depths of depravity by demons who have overpowered the human spirit and driven it mad with evil desires. The only way such people will ever be helped is for some

Christian to take authority over these demons and cast them out in the name of Jesus.

Finally, we came to the Doon Doon spirit. This was the last of them. I learned that this spirit had been driving the woman to commit suicide. The urge had been so strong that, at times, she had almost been driven to insanity.

"Doon Doon, you spirit of suicide," I said, "I command you to come out of this woman this very moment. In the name of Jesus, hold your peace and come out."

Instantly, I saw her relax. It was very noticeable, because she had been so tense and tormented throughout the meeting. But now, suddenly, an expression of calm smoothed out her features. She looked up at me. I can never forget the sight of those dark brown eyes and that brown face, and her little hands lifted toward me.

"I want to know your Jesus, too," she said, tears trickling down her cheeks. It was my great joy to introduce her to Jesus, and she opened up and received Him joyfully. What a miracle!

I learned later that her name was Habigan Adool, and that she was a Moslem who had been bound by demon spirits for eight of her 25 years. She was married to a man who had recently become a Christian. Although he knew that his wife was in very serious condition, he did not understand the cause of her problem. In desperation, he had sought help

195

for her from almost any source which seemed to offer even a glimmer of hope. He had taken her to a psychiatrist. He had taken her to a medical doctor. He had even taken her to the witch doctor and the Hindu priest. None of them had been able to help her.

But Jesus made the difference. A short time after I left the island, I received a report of Habigan's receiving the baptism in the Holy Spirit. Her husband could hardly believe the difference in her!

On the way home, as I thought back over my trips to Kenya, Jamaica and Trinidad, I asked myself, "What am I doing in America, when there are so many afflicted and oppressed people in other lands who are craving to hear the Gospel, and wanting to be free? In America, we can hear the Gospel on the radio almost any time of day. We can see it on television. We can go to church almost any day of the week. We've preached the Gospel so much that many of our people have hardened their hearts and are not responding to God's call. But in many other countries they hunger and thirst for this message."

When I got back to Tacoma, there was Stella at the airport, a gaunt figure trying to stand strong. One look at her, and I knew there could be no more trips. She needed care, and I made up my mind to ride out the storm with her.

About that time, I received a pastoral call to the Open Bible Chapel in Vancouver, British Columbia. Immediately, I sensed this was God's leading. The congregation in Vancouver was smaller than my congregation in Tacoma. There would be fewer demands on me, and I would have more time to spend with Stella. So in the spring of 1965 we moved to Canada, and the little church at Vancouver became a place of shelter for us during the stormy months ahead.

So convinced was Stella that God was going to heal her that she said one day, "Andrew, I'm going to knit myself a coat. It won't be long until I'll be traveling to the mission fields with you, and I'll need this coat to wear when it is cool in the evenings."

She sat there knitting constantly, and she'd talk about the next missionary trip, when she'd be with me. It gave me a sick feeling, as I thought within myself, "Honey, it's never going to be."

But never once did she falter. She was still the same jovial, talkative person she'd always been. She insisted on traveling with me to any special services I had within driving distance. I made her as comfortable as I could in the car, and took her along. In the services she would testify of her faith in God's healing power, and her beaming face was an inspiration to everyone. Little did the people know of the pain she was suffering.

Sometimes we attended healing services together. She was prayed for by many outstanding evangelists who had been greatly used in this kind of ministry. But nothing ever happened. Still, her faith remained unshaken. She was just the same the day she entered the Lion's Gate Hospital in Vancouver.

"Andrew," she said, "don't you worry. God's going to heal me; just you wait and see." Before I left her that evening, we prayed together again—and, oh, what faith she had! I left the room rejoicing at the simplicity of her childlike trust.

But she continued to get worse. The boys came and stayed for a few days at a time. We didn't say much about it, but all of us realized that her time was not long. Philip decided that I shouldn't be alone during those days, so he remained with me in our little apartment.

The doctor whispered to me one day, "My! That woman of yours! She should have been dead months ago. I don't know what's keeping her alive, but it must be her strong faith in God!"

The nurses noticed too. She was always telling them about the Lord, always smiling. They said, "That woman is a miracle!"

On Thursday morning, November 25, 1965, Philip and I went up to the hospital very early. The tubes protruding from Stella's side and the bottles beside her bed were now a familiar sight. She was noticeably weaker.

"Andrew," she said, "I'm going to be healed today. Take these tubes out of my side."

"But Stella," I said, "what will the nurses say if I do that?"

"It doesn't matter," she replied, "I'm going to get out of this bed and prove to God that I've got faith in His healing power!"

I knew she meant well. "Stella," I said kindly, "you don't have to prove anything to God by taking those tubes out. God can heal you with the tubes in. You don't have to get out of bed just to prove your faith to God. If He wants to heal you, just accept it where you are."

She finally agreed that we'd be in big trouble if we tampered with those tubes. So she relaxed and began to rest her faith in God for the outcome.

We stayed with her all day, and tried to tend to her needs as faithfully as we could. The doctors and nurses came and went quietly, and the day wore on. By the time the sun went down that evening, she was unconscious. We called her name over and over, but there was no reply. But still we prayed on, and I kept thinking about what she had said concerning being healed that day. About 10 o'clock that evening, she slipped away peacefully and went home to be with God . . . .

For a fleeting moment, there came the

thought, "But God can raise her from the dead." And we prayed that if it was God's will, it would happen. But the doctors came, and the nurses, and in a few moments the curtains were drawn around her bed.

When Philip and I left her room, I remembered the vision I'd had in Jamaica. God had been good to reveal His will to me, although it was a secret she never knew. She had wanted to travel with me so badly. But God had something better for her than being with me on the mission field.

As we stepped out into the cold night, I wiped the tears from my eyes, looked up into the heavens and said under my breath, "Stella, God healed you today . . . ."

CHAPTER SIXTEEN

The Invisible Wall

A few months after Stella's home-going, I finished up my assignment at Vancouver, and moved to San Diego, California. There was no question in my mind now that God was steering me in a new direction, and that much of my time would be spent overseas. I had been managing the work of the Independent Assemblies of God International for a number of years, and my responsibilities had grown until it was now a major assignment.

San Diego seemed like a good base of operations for the Assemblies, although I knew that much of my time would need to be spent away from the office. My official duties must not replace my soul-winning ministry. The mantle had fallen on me, as on many others. The Holy Spirit was being poured out everywhere. Many of the mainline churches in the States were showing encouraging signs of new life. We were hearing constant reports of revival from many of our mission stations, and receiving endless calls for help.

"God," I said, "there's such a shortage of manpower. People overseas are literally *crying* out for the Gospel. There are great areas where one man must serve thousands upon thousands of people. It seems that we just don't have enough people to do the job. What's wrong?"

I had met many younger people who seemed eager enough to preach the Gospel abroad, but for some reason they weren't getting there. Practically every missionary I met was begging for more help, but very little help was coming. As I prayed, God brought to my mind a vision He had given me back in November of 1952. It happened while I was doing my second pastorate at the Philadelphia Church in Chicago.

We were living in a mobile home in the northwest suburbs. Around 5 in the morning, I woke up and couldn't get back to sleep.

"Well," I thought, "it's foolish to be wasting time lying in bed. As long as I'm awake, I might as well get up and read the Bible."

I got up quietly, dressed and went out to

the kitchen table to read. After a short time, I felt a strong urge to pray, so I pulled the chair away from the table, and knelt there in worship. God's presence was powerful that morning; it was good to be at His feet in adoration. But then, very unexpectedly, a vision appeared before my eyes. It was as distinct and clear as though I were seeing a picture on a television screen.

I was standing before a great unnamed cathedral. Its stately spires tapered up into the sky like poised missiles. Its Gothic arches were graceful and strong. The walls were reinforced with sturdy buttresses and the windows were made of intricately designed stained glass. Every stone in that building was pure granite, and I thought of the vast amount of money which must have been necessary to build such an edifice. What a masterpiece of workmanship it was! But as I gazed at this great cathedral, a voice spoke:

"My son," the Voice began, "people say, 'What a beautiful church!' But I say unto you, this is not MY church!"

I jumped ahead of Him, and thought I knew what He was going to say next. But then the vision changed.

I saw myself standing on a street in a great cit overseas. It was early in the morning. The streets were made of cobblestone. Wobbly two-wheeled carts loaded with produce were rattling down the streets, the owners perched atop, on their way to the market. The streets were in very bad condition. Many of the stones were out of place, others almost totally covered with mud. In some places there were great mudholes. Some of the curbstones were knocked into the street. As I walked along that street, noticing these miserable cobblestones, I was amazed to hear voices speaking out of those stones!

"Come! Oh, come!" they cried. "Come and build us into the temple of the Lord!" They called very pitifully, as though in great distress.

Then my attention was drawn to a far horizon. There, in the distance, I saw men of God coming to answer the cry of those poor old cobblestones. Many of them were coming, intent on plucking those old stones out of the mire and building them into God's temple. They were running with all their might to answer the call of the cobblestones.

But then I saw that something was hindering them. There seemed to be an invisible wall, and they could come just so far, and no further. They tried and tried to get past that wall. They pushed against it; they tried to knock it over; they tried to climb over it. But none succeeded.

"How strange!" I thought. "They want to come, but they can't. I wonder what is hindering them?" Then the Lord began to speak to me distinctly and clearly.

204

"I will explain the last part of the vision to you first," He said. "The cobblestones in the mire represent the millions who have not yet heard the word of salvation. Year after year, they live in their sins with none to help them. If someone would only take the message of salvation to them, they would become 'living stones' in the Church I am building."

I remembered some of the missionary magazines I had read, and recalled the pictures of thousands upon thousands of black and brown people without Christ.

"I am now pouring out of My Spirit upon many of my servants," the Lord continued. "My Church is being clothed with gifts and power, and shall be restored to beauty and glory. But even though many are anointed with power and many are hearing the call of the cobblestones, yet they are hindered from answering the call. Before my Church can be restored to her full glory, she must learn the mystery of the invisible wall."

"Please tell me," I begged, "that I may tell your people what it is that hinders."

"Here is understanding," He said. "My anointed servants are hindered by lack of funds. The tithe belongs to them. I have appointed it to them for their use. But my people have used the tithes for building great temples and cathedrals, and paying architects. They say, 'What beautiful churches we have built for God!' They rob my anointed ser-

vants of the tithes, and use them instead to pay off mortgages and interest. And my Church goes unbuilt for lack of funds."

I hadn't expected that. The church I was serving at that time was quite large, and we taught all of our people that God expected them to give at least a tenth of their money to God. Of course, some people accused me of preaching Old Testament Law. One evangelist, who disagreed with my position, started calling us "ten-cent Christians." But I figured that a dime was better than a nickel any day, and continued to teach our people to give ten per cent. The argument that tithing belongs to the Law was not valid, because I knew that tithing was practiced long before the Law was ever given, both by Abraham and by Jacob.

But God wasn't talking to me about *giving* tithes; He was talking about how they are to be *disbursed*. And we, like many other churches, had been using the tithe fund for quite a number of purposes. There was a long list of things: my weekly salary, support of missionaries, mortgage and interest payments, building maintenance, light and heat, the sexton's salary. And if I understood God correctly, He was saying that the tithe was to be used *only* for the support of the ministry.

"But Lord," I protested, "if we give all the tithe to the ministry, how are we going to meet all these other expenses? Who will make

the mortgage payments? Who will buy the literature? Who will pay for the utilities?"

"*My son,*" He said without hesitation, "*if you will do what I tell you, and obey the voice of My Spirit, I will bless you and multiply your ministry until multitudes will be saved. And as I move upon them by My Spirit, they will gladly give love offerings which will be more than sufficient for all these other needs. But you must use the tithe as I have shown you.*" And with that, the vision disappeared.

Well! I was really in a predicament! I simply didn't have the courage even to suggest it to my church board. In fact, I wasn't even sure I *wanted* to. I made it an earnest matter of prayer, however, and began to search the scriptures to make sure the vision was really from God. I had learned a long time ago that visions are not to be trusted unless they are scriptural.

I had studied the subject of tithing many times before, but this time I was looking for something different. How is the tithe to be disbursed? That was the big question. The first verse that I noticed was Leviticus 27:30:

And all the tithe of the land, whether of the seed of the land, or of the fruit of the tree, is the Lord's: it is holy unto the Lord.

"Why," I thought, "if the tithe is the Lord's, then nobody else has any right to say how it shall be disbursed. It *belongs* to Him. It is His to use as He sees fit."

I had no sooner left that verse than the Holy Spirit led me to another one in Numbers 18:21:

And, behold, I have given the children of Levi all the tenth in Israel for an inheritance, for their service which they serve, even the service of the tabernacle of the congregation.

I read and re-read those words. "I have given . . . I have given the children of Levi all the tenth . . . all the tenth . . . all the tenth." Of course! How could I have missed that before? The tithe is the Lord's to use as He chooses, and He chooses to give it *all* to His ministers!

"Well, Lord," I said, "we haven't done it that way. We've used the tithe for many other things in addition to the ministry. But here, Lord, You are saying that all of the tithe is Yours and You have a right to do with it what You want to do, and You have given the tithe to Your ministers."

So who was I to argue? Why, if *I* went away on a trip and gave a man $1,000 to disburse for me while I was gone, wouldn't I have a right to expect him to follow my directions? I would say, "I want you to disburse this money this way: so much for utilities, so much for rent, so much for repairs." I would itemize every foreseeable expense. But if I came back from my trip and found that the man had spent the money as he pleased, and that the utilities weren't paid and the rent wasn't paid, wouldn't I be disturbed? Certainly I would—I would have a right to be. So I began to see how God must feel when we disburse the tithe as we please, and not according to His will. If He has given the tithes to the Levites for the services they render to the congregation, will He be pleased if we use the money for the building and repairing of church buildings, or the paying of mortgages?

I leaned back in my chair and stared out the office window for a moment. I knew that if I tried to apply this principle to my church, there would be a great controversy raised. In fact, I wouldn't dare suggest such an idea unless I could first show them from the Word of God that the idea was scriptural. I would have to teach them patiently, until they could see what I was seeing—whatever it was that I was seeing!

A few days later, I returned to the subject again. Much of my preaching about tithing had been taken from the book of Malachi, so I decided to see if I could find any further light on the subject by going through that little book again. I had just gotten started into chapter 1, when my attention was arrested by a passage starting at verse 6, where God was rebuking the priests of Israel for the dishonorable way they were doing His work. When I came to verses 7 and 8, I could almost feel the anger in God's voice:

Ye offer polluted bread upon mine altar: and ye say, . . . The table of the Lord is contemptible.

. . . if ye offer the blind for sacrifice, is it not evil? and if ye offer the lame and sick, is it not evil? offer it now unto thy governor; will he be pleased with thee, or accept thy person? saith the Lord of hosts.

I began to wonder why the priests would offer contemptible sacrifices to God. After all, the sacrificial meat was God's provision for them. A part of every sacrifice was given to the priests so that they could enjoy barbecued beef and roast mutton. It would seem that they would have been more careful to offer only grade A meat on God's altar! But then I read verse 14:

But cursed be the deceiver, which hath in his flock a male, and voweth, and sacrificeth unto the Lord a corrupt thing . . . .

Instantly, I saw the problem. The priests had nothing to offer to God except that which was given to them by the people. And what were the people giving? They were giving blind sheep, lame calves and sick turtledoves. In my imagination, I could see the whole problem being acted out before me.

I could see a selfish man going out to his

herds to pick a sheep for God. There are hun-
dreds of sheep milling around, and he can
hardly hear himself thinking for their noisy
bleating.

"Hmmmm," he says, "poor old Becky's got
T.B., and she's so skinny she's no good to me
anymore. I guess I'll give her to the priests."

And so he takes the poor straggly thing
down to the temple, and they butcher her for
sacrifice. And when the priests sit down to eat
their part, one of them says, "I can't eat this
stuff! Didn't you see how sick this sheep was
when it was brought in?" And the others too
turn away in disgust.

"Why don't they bring us something de-
cent?" one asks.

"How utterly contemptible!"

Of course, that was no excuse for the
priests. They should have refused such offerings and taught the people to give what God
required. But, be that as it may, I could see
that it was a double-barreled problem. Small
wonder that many of the priests were turning
away from ministering in the Temple. The
tithe that God had appointed them was being
withheld, and instead they were receiving offerings that were torn, lame and sick.

Then it occurred to me that I had seen a
good many modern counterparts of this same
problem in my travels. I had spoken in many
churches and met quite a number of pastors
who were having a difficult time making ends

meet. I could almost see the scene before my eyes, because it had been related to me so many times, with a few variations.

"You know, Honey," Brother Brown says to his wife, "I think our pastor needs a new refrigerator."

"What makes you think so?" she inquires.

"Well, I stopped over at his house yesterday to return those books I borrowed from him, and his wife has to set the milk out in the snow to keep it cold. She said something about the refrigerator not working very well."

"Oh, isn't that too bad!" she replies sadly. "And the pastor doesn't draw much salary either."

"Well, I'm going to do something about it," he says, beaming. "I've been thinking for some time that we ought to get ourselves a new refrigerator, so why don't we give our old one to the pastor? The motor's getting pretty noisy and it vibrates a good deal, but at least it keeps the food cold, and it would be better than the one he has."

"Oh, John," she says, "that's a wonderful idea!"

So they go down to the appliance store the next day and buy themselves a brand new General Electric refrigerator with a frost-free freezer compartment. It's just the right color to match the rest of the kitchen, and Mrs. Brown is delighted with it.

"We certainly needed it," she says. "Isn't it gorgeous?"

Then Brother Brown stops over at the pastor's house. "Pastor," he says, "I noticed that your refrigerator is just about worn out." [It hasn't worked at all for six months.] "And since the Mrs. and I just bought ourselves a new refrigerator, we'd like to give you our old one. If you'll just arrange to pick it up, it's yours for the hauling away." [. . . which is a convenient way to get rid of the old hunk of junk.]

So the young pastor and his wife appear very grateful, and they thank the man profusely for his kindness. Of course, they would have been able to buy a new refrigerator long ago if only Brother Brown and a few others like him had been setting aside their tithes for their pastor, instead of pouring so much money into the church building program.

No sooner had that picture faded from my mind, than I recalled another familiar scene.

"Sarah," Brother Jones says to his wife, "do you know that our pastor has been wearing that same suit ever since he came to our church four years ago?"

"Yes, Jim," she says, "it's getting pretty threadbare, isn't it?"

"I've got an idea," he says. "He's about my size, you know, and I'm tired of my old suit, so I think I'll give it to the pastor and go buy myself a new one."

213

*So he goes down to the nearby men's cloth-
ing store and picks out one of the latest-fash-
ion suits for himself. In a few days, he's over
knocking on the pastor's door.*

*"Pastor," he says cheerfully, "I've been
noticing that you could use a new suit, and
I've got an old one here that's still serviceable.
I think God wants me to give it to you." [But
God wouldn't wish that suit on a scarecrow.]*

*But the pastor smiles and replies, "Brother
Jones, you shouldn't have done it!" [... which
is probably true.]*

I thought quietly for a few minutes, and
then returned to my Bible. I read Malachi
1:8 over again:

*"... if ye offer the blind for sacrifice, is it
not evil? and if ye offer the lame and sick ...
[or the worn out and threadbare] is it not evil?
offer it now unto thy governor; will he be
pleased with thee, or accept thy person? saith
the Lord of hosts.*

It was becoming more and more clear to me
that, at least in Old Testament times, God
had a definite plan for disbursing the tithe. *All*
the tithe belonged to the anointed ministers
of the Temple. But I still wasn't sure whether
this principle applied to New Testament
Christians. All of the information I had found
so far was from the Old Testament. So I began to search the pages of the New Testament.

I knew I was on the right track when I

found that passage beginning in 1 Corinthians 9:7:

Who goeth a warfare any time at his own charges? who planteth a vineyard and eateth not of the fruit thereof? or who feedeth a flock, and eateth not of the milk of the flock? ... For it is written in the law of Moses, Thou shalt not muzzle the mouth of the ox that treadeth out the corn. Doth God take care for oxen? Or saith he it altogether for our sakes? For our sakes, no doubt, this is written: that he that ploweth should plow in hope; and that he that thresheth in hope should be partaker of his hope. If we have sown unto you spiritual things, is it a great thing if we shall reap your carnal things?

This seemed quite clear to me. God was saying that every man has a right to live by the fruit of his own labors. A soldier has a right to expect his government to pay him. The gardener has a right to eat his own produce. The dairyman has a right to drink his cows' milk.

Even in Old Testament times God had told them that they were not to muzzle the ox that treads out the corn. If you expect an ox to work for you all day, then the ox has a right to eat some of the corn. And it seemed obvious to me that this same principle applied to New Testament ministers of the Gospel. Any man who devotes his life to the spiritual welfare of others ought to be taken care of materially by those to whom he ministers. This must have been what Paul meant when he said, "If we have sown unto you spiritual things, is it a great thing if we shall reap your carnal [or material] things?"

I was pretty sure I had found what I was looking for. I didn't see how it could be stated much more clearly than this. But then I came to verses 13 and 14:

Do ye not know that they which minister about holy things live of the things of the temple? and they which wait at the altar are partakers with the altar? Even so hath the Lord ordained that they which preach the gospel should live of the gospel.

I just about jumped out of my chair. "Lord," I shouted, "that's *IT!* That's the answer!"

I read it again. Here God was using the Old Testament priesthood as an example of how the New Testament ministry is to be cared for. The tithes belonged to the priests, and they lived on those tithes. They ate the meat and the bread. They drank the wine. And it didn't cost them a cent. God had decreed that the tithe belonged to the Levites, and it was theirs to use. And now, in like manner, God had decreed in these New Testament times that they which preach the Gospel should live of the Gospel.

I felt like a Moses on the mount who had just received a great revelation. But what a revolutionary revelation! I had visited many churches where the pastor was the lowest paid man in the congregation. I knew of many underpaid pastors who were ministering to businessmen earning $50,000 a year or more. Many of these businessmen were contributing heavily to their churches, but their churches did not understand that the tithe belonged to the ministry; therefore they spent it on construction programs and building maintenance, while the pastor received just enough to get along on. I saw the problem all too clearly.

With fear and trembling, I began to teach this new concept to my congregation. I found out at the board meeting just how revolutionary the idea was! Not wanting to risk unnecessary misunderstanding, I dropped the subject and began instead to share my findings with a few select people I met in my travels.

"That's ridiculous!" one man said. "If we give all out tithes to the pastor, he'll get too much!"

"Well, it might seem that way," I said, "but you must remember that the priests of the Old Testament didn't use all of the tithes personally. They went to the storehouses and took out *what they needed*."

"You mean, then, that the pastor should be

able to draw out of the tithe fund whatever he feels he honestly needs?"

"Exactly!"

"But what if he draws out *more* than he needs?"

"What! Can't you trust your pastor? If you can't trust him, he's not worthy to *be* your pastor."

"Maybe you're right."

I was sure I was. After all, it wasn't my idea, was it? God had shown me the idea in a vision and then confirmed it by the Scriptures. Who was I to resist God?

Finally God made it plain that He *expected* me to share this teaching with the churches of our fellowship. Obviously, some would reject it—but others would accept. *My* responsibility was to share the message. So I began to teach all about God's plan for us to experience restoration to New Testament order not only in spiritual things, but in material things as well. The plan was very simple. Each local church could establish a tithe fund, and all moneys would be kept in that one fund and earmarked for the ministry. The pastor would draw *agreed-upon* amounts from that fund, according to his needs. If the entire amount were honestly needed by the pastor, then he should be free to use the entire fund. If there were funds left over, then the surplus would be designated for other ministries.

For instance, if a local church wanted to

start a branch ministry in a suburb or a neighboring community, there would be no problem about expenses. If a young man from the church felt called of God to oversee such a ministry, the "mother church" could say to him, "All right, you go and get that work established and we'll take care of you. You don't need to worry. We'll support you until you get that congregation built up. After you teach them to tithe and support you, we'll withdraw our tithe and start another branch somewhere else."

I was absolutely convinced that this was God's way of multiplying and expanding His kingdom. Following this simple plan, any congregation could saturate a whole city for God, and even reach into foreign lands. All they had to do was set aside the *whole tithe* for the ministry. I had seen more than enough of the results of a poorly supported ministry. I had seen little struggling churches where the pastor barely existed, while large portions of the tithe were being used to pay for utilities, denominational assessments, college funds, roof repairs, painting Sunday School rooms and buying literature. I knew this was absolutely the wrong way of doing it. I saw clearly that the tithe of the congregation belonged to the ministry of that congregation—every single penny of it. And I knew that if this simple principle were followed, the local ministry would be properly cared for, and missionaries and evangelists could be supported as well.

But there was still one more question bothering me. Ever since 1944, I had been serving as secretary of the Independent Assemblies of God International, which is the highest office in that fellowship. In that position, it was my responsibility to oversee the work of the fellowship and assist in whatever ways I could. This involved much traveling and expense.

"What," I wondered, "is the scriptural way of supporting a ministry like this?" Up until that time, I had simply been receiving a love offering each time I spoke in a church, and that was usually sufficient to meet my needs. But now I had a hunch that God had a better plan, so I took my Bible and began hunting for the answer. I finally found what I was looking for in the book of Numbers.

In chapter 18, I found special instructions given to the Levites about how *they* were to tithe. The Levites, of course, had no income other than the tithes of the people. *All* the tithe was theirs. And here were instructions about how they were to *tithe their tithes!* I read verse 26 with a great deal of interest:

Thus speak unto the Levites, and say unto them, When ye take of the children of Israel

*the tithes which I have given you from them
for your inheritance, then ye shall offer up an
heave offering of it for the Lord, even a tenth
part of the tithe.*

So at least that much was very plain. The
Levites *did* give away a tenth of the tithes.
Having read in I Corinthians 9:9, 10 that
these Old Testament principles were written
for the sake of New Testament believers, I
concluded that this was a basis for believing
that ministers ought to give a tenth of their
tithe. But to whom? Should a pastor simply
take his tenth and put it back into the tithe
fund of his church? This is what I had been
doing up until that time. But if the tithe *belongs* to the ministry, then I was simply giving a tenth back to myself! I knew that
couldn't be God's way. The Levites obviously
did not dedicate a tenth of their tithe to God,
and then turn right around and put it back
into the storehouse!

So I read on down a few verses, and certain
words in verse 28 almost leaped off the
page:

*Thus ye also shall offer an heave offering
unto the Lord of all your tithes, which ye receive of the children of Israel; and ye shall
give thereof the Lord's heave offering to Aaron
the priest.*

There it was! The Levites tithed to Aaron.
The priests tithed to the High Priest who was

over them. In New Testament terms, that would simply mean that *ministers and pastors ought to give their tenth to the ministry which is over them.*

So I began, in seminars and conventions, to share this teaching with our pastors, showing them God's plan for the financing of our fellowship. I tried to show them how much more effective our work could be if we had an adequately financed overseeing ministry. Of course, I knew that I could do no more than point out what I had seen in the Word of God. No attempt was made to impose this principle on our pastors as a matter of legislation. We were not a denomination, and I had no desire to legislate anything. The only purpose of our organization was fellowship and helpfulness. All of our churches were self-governing groups. My function as an overseer was simply to give help and share scriptural insights as they were needed. We often gathered together in conventions for this purpose.

Little by little, some of the brethren of our fellowship began to understand the principle of giving a tenth of their tithe to the overseeing ministry. Soon the money began to come in. I proceeded to set this money aside in a special fund, and whenever some trip needed to be made in the interest of our fellowship, I would keep careful records and give reports of receipts and expenditures at the annual conventions. As a result, I was able to travel more and more and have a far more effective ministry in opening up new frontiers for Christ. I also began to receive reports of some of our churches adopting the whole plan of setting aside the tithe for the ministry. It was working!

The plan was fantastically simple and beautiful. The people tithe to the ministry; the ministers tithe to the overseeing minister. And in both cases, there is more than enough. The local church finds it has enough to support the pastor, plus a great deal left over for branch ministries and new frontiers, while God provides for all other material needs. And as the pastors respond with a tenth of their tithe to the overseeing minister, *he* discovers that there is more than enough for *his* expenses too, and he is able to pass the excess money on to new missionaries who want to answer God's call but have no means of support.

When I thought all this over, I knew I had unraveled the mystery of the invisible wall. The men of God I had seen in the vision could have been mightily used of God. They could have been down there in the streets of that great city, lifting those "cobblestones" out of the mire and building them into the Church of the Living God. But the invisible wall of misused tithes prevented them . . . .

I dropped back into 1966 with a jolt. Here I was in my office in San Diego, asking God why there was such a shortage of workers. And *that* was the answer! It came to me more forcibly than ever that the Lord had given me another key to the restoration of the Church. It wasn't enough that thousands upon thousands of people were being swept into the kingdom of God. It wasn't enough that God was raising up a great army of Spirit-filled witnesses, equipped with the gifts of the Spirit. What good is an army, if there isn't sufficient money to mobilize it? Will Satan be defeated by an army that can't reach the battle front?

"God," I said, "I promise you, this message will be preached and published around the world. Your people must have this key."

CHAPTER SEVENTEEN

Getting Back in Gear

It was in 1966 that I met Ruth. I had been invited to a convention to be held in San Diego.

Among the many friends I saw there was R. L. Davis, pastor of the Central Assembly of God in El Cajon, a suburb of San Diego.

"Brother Rasmussen," he said to me one day, drawing a big breath, "we've been friends for a good many years . . . ."

"Yes, we have."

"Well, what I have to say is rather personal, but I thought . . . ."

"It's all right," I assured him. "What's on your mind?"

"Well, I was just thinking that it's been some time now since Stella passed away."

"Yes."

"It must be terribly lonely."

"It is."

"Brother Rasmussen," he said, "would you be interested in meeting a good Christian woman?"

"Well," I said, "maybe . . . ."

Some time later, he came back with Ruth. She was a member of his church, and her husband had passed away some 4 years before. After being introduced, we enjoyed a pleasant time of conversation. We also found further opportunities during the convention to chat and enjoy fellowship.

After the convention, we continued to correspond and saw each other occasionally. However, both of us were very cautious. In the first place, there were the gossipers who would think I was forming another friendship too soon after Stella's death, no matter how long I waited. Furthermore, Ruth had no intentions of getting married again. So for a while, it was merely a pleasant friendship.

As time went on, though, we both began to think more seriously about the possibility of marriage. In many ways, it seemed like a good idea. Ruth liked the idea of sharing with me in the ministry, and R. L. Davis, "the matchmaker," thought we were a perfect combination.

Well, it did seem that God had caused our paths to cross very providentially, and the more I thought about it, the more I began to

226

have a sense of divine guidance. But I wanted to be absolutely sure we were doing the right thing, so I began praying for some additional guidance.

"Lord," I prayed, "if you want me to marry Ruth, you must indicate it to me in some special way." I left the matter in God's hands, sure that He would give some very clear guidance one way or another.

Months later I was speaking at Arrowhead Camp in the State of Minnesota. One of the other speakers was Bryn Jones, an English missionary from British Guiana, South America. I had been greatly blessed by his ministry throughout the camp meeting. One morning, the Spirit of God came upon him and he began to prophesy, and God's message came to me with unmistakable authority: *"My servant Rasmussen, I know the woman you have in mind for marriage. Do not be afraid to take her unto you as your wife, for she is an appointed vessel to be your helper."*

I was amazed. That missionary knew absolutely *nothing* about my friendship with Ruth.

Now I certainly do *not* advocate getting married simply because someone prophesies that you should. But this had definite marks of being genuine. In the first place, I already had a sense of divine guidance; I only wanted a confirmation of what I already felt. Secondly, the message came through a mature, dedicated servant of the Lord. Thirdly, this servant knew nothing of my need; yet he spoke to me with authority. Furthermore, I felt a great witness of the Holy Spirit as he spoke.

"All right, Lord," I thought, "if this is Your will, I will proceed."

I went back to San Diego, and on June 3, 1967—a year and a half after we first met—Ruth and I were married in the Assembly of God Church in El Cajon. During the ceremony, Pastor R. L. Davis gave an unusual prophetic utterance regarding God's blessing on our marriage and how God was going to use us together. It looked as though God had set the stage for a new phase of my life. I now had my eye on a much greater ministry, and it was obvious that Ruth was to have some part in it.

Our first trip was to South America. I marveled at Ruth's simple faith, and how God used her to minister healing to many sick people.

"Lord," I said gratefully, "thank You for such a good companion to help me in my ministry!" We came back from South America tired, but happy to be working together.

In 1970, I made a trip to Haiti to conduct a ten-day crusade. After a great deal of prayer, Ruth decided not to go along on this trip. The swing through South America had been exhausting. However, she was looking forward to traveling with me again on subsequent trips.

The crusade in Haiti was to be a massive effort. We had rented an open-air location which would accommodate twenty to thirty thousand people. When I arrived, however, I found there had been a great deal of agitation taking place on the island because of some Communist activities, and that the President of the island had issued an order that there would be no more open-air meetings until the uprising was quelled.

Even so, I was sure that God had sent me for a very definite purpose. I was there to preach the message of salvation, to heal the sick, and to lay hands on Christians for the baptism in the Spirit; I was there to teach the national pastors about God's plan for the restoration of the Church in these last days. I knew the quickest way to evangelize any land is to teach the native pastors how to develop strong self-supporting churches. My mission was of utmost importance.

With that in mind, I searched for a building to rent. I finally found an open-roofed theater which would seat around three or four thousand people, and I was able to rent it for our crusade.

I had requested that arrangements be made

to bring as many pastors as possible to our daytime meetings. We paid no attention to denomination. Our only thought was to get our message out to anyone who would listen. We planned to have sessions for the pastors every day from 10 in the morning until 2 in the afternoon, or later. We also had a team of some of our faithful pastors to help with the teaching: Pastor Lawrenson from Canada, Pastor Bender from Florida, Pastor Bowan from Wyoming, and Pastor Gamble from Pennsylvania, along with a number of others. I was the one who would speak in the evening meetings to the thousands who would jam into that open-roofed theater. We were all set for an exciting ten days. The only problem remaining was the weather.

Though it was the dry season, it had been raining ever since the first day we arrived. Still, we had been going ahead with our plans, in faith that God would take care of the rain when the time came.

"Brother Rasmussen," the local missionary, Nick Gruick said, "this is highly unusual. It just doesn't rain at this time of year. If this rain keeps up, it's going to keep our crowds down."

"Maybe they'll come even in the rain," I suggested.

"No," Nick said, "the Haitians will not come out when it rains because they're not accustomed to wet weather at this time of year.

They would not want to expose themselves to the unnecessary danger of colds."

So I went over to our theater to size up the situation again. There was a small segment of roof over the rear of the building, which covered the camera room and a few of the balcony seats in the rear. But the rest was entirely open. The stage and all of the cement seats were exposed to the weather, and the rain was falling steadily.

"Lord," I prayed, as I stood there, "if you don't stop this rain, a lot of Your money will go down the drain." The crusade was an expensive project for our fellowship. Renting the theater was expensive enough. But we were also responsible to provide housing and food for the national pastors who were coming in from all parts of the island. Haiti was an island of extreme poverty, and the pastors wouldn't have been able to come if we had not paid their way. There was an outlay of thousands of dollars in order to make this crusade possible. I remember now that I had a sick feeling in the pit of my stomach at the mere thought of losing that much money. I thought of the people in our fellowship who had given to make this mission possible. "Wouldn't it be terrible if . . .?"

But then I scolded myself. "What's the matter with you?" I said. "Is God dead?" I walked back to Nick's home, planning to move into the crusade on schedule.

The morning of the first day was beautiful. We had scheduled a fellowship breakfast for the pastors, and they came from everywhere for the meeting. God seemed to hover near; we all sensed that the crusade would be something very special.

But by late afternoon, the sun had disappeared. Heavy, lead-gray clouds were hanging low over the city, and rain was threatening. In fact, I noticed that a few drops were already falling. I looked at my watch. It was only a short time until the evening meeting would begin, and it looked as though all our plans were to be washed away. I anxiously watched the heavy clouds from the window of Nick's livingroom.

"Jesus," I prayed, "I know you can stop the rain . . . ."

"*You stop it*," He said.

"Who, me?"

"*Yes*," He said. "*Have I not said to you, 'The works that I do shall ye do also, and greater works than these shall ye do, because I go to my Father'?*"

I'm not sure which surprised me more—the greatness of that promise, or the smallness of my faith. I remembered how Jesus had taken authority over the weather on one occasion, and stilled a storm. Now He was saying that I could do the works *He* did. So I went outside and looked up into the face of those threatening clouds.

"You clouds," I said in a loud voice, "in the name of Jesus, I command you to seal up and not send a drop of rain over this city tonight." Then, as an act of faith, I began to thank the Lord for hearing and answering my prayer.

About 10 minutes later, Nick and I drove down to the meeting in the Volkswagen van. It was early, but the crowds were already filling up the building. By the time I stepped out on the stage of that theater to begin the service, night had fallen over the island. The first sight that greeted my eyes was several thousand black faces; but then I couldn't help but look up through the open roof. There was a clear sky—the heavens were star-spangled, and the moon was glimmering in the distance. Not a drop of rain fell that night. The words of Jesus to Martha came to me very forcefully: *"Said I not unto thee, that, if thou wouldest believe, thou shouldest see the glory of God?"* (John 11:40)

With glorious weather during the rest of the ten-day crusade, the crowds increased at each meeting. Hundreds were saved, many were baptized in the Holy Spirit, and many were healed. On the closing day, at the ten o'clock seminar, there were approximately

250 pastors present, representing many different denominations.

"How many here would like to be baptized in the Holy Spirit?" I asked, fully aware there were some in the group who wouldn't agree with this teaching at all. Forty-nine hands went up.

"How wonderful!" I thought, and proceeded to explain to them how to enter into this deeper relationship with Jesus.

"Of course, you know that *I* cannot baptize you," I told them. "Nor can anyone else who is here. Only Jesus can do this for you. *He* shall baptize you with the Holy Ghost and with fire."

Then I went on and explained to them about the ministry of laying on of hands. "When Peter and John laid their hands on the Samaritans," I said, "they were baptized in the Holy Spirit. Now this is certainly not the *only* way to receive this experience, but it is *one* way. One Spirit-filled Christian may lay his hands on another Christian, and that Christian too will become filled. Not that any man has the power to impart the Holy Ghost. But Jesus, who is the Baptizer, often channels His power through people. That's what happened at Samaria. Peter and John laid their hands on the Samaritans, and Jesus allowed the Spirit which was in them to flow into the Samaritans also. That very same miracle can happen to you now. I will lay my hands on you as Peter did. I cannot give you the Holy Spirit, but if you are sincere in your desires, then Jesus will allow the Holy Spirit which is in me to flow into you, and you will receive the Holy Spirit by the laying on of hands."

Then I asked some of the other pastors and missionaries to join with me and, one by one, we laid our hands on every one of those pastors who wanted to be baptized in the Spirit. Each one began to speak in tongues, and we knew that Jesus was doing His work. It was wonderful to be there.

"How many of you who raised your hands before have now been baptized in the Holy Spirit?" I asked when it was all over.

The hands were lifted again, and we counted them. There were fifty. Apparently, one more had been encouraged to come for prayer when he saw the others receiving.

Some time after returning to the States, I received a letter from Nick Gruick, the missionary who had arranged our crusade. "Brother Rasmussen," he wrote, "since you left, these pastors have been coming to our meetings here in Port-au-Prince. There have been as many as 500 who have been baptized in the Spirit."

"Lord," I prayed, "how can I ever thank You enough?" I knew that He had led me to Haiti; and even though my stay had been short, great things were continuing to be accomplished. It seemed that His seal of approval was upon this "barnstorming missionary ministry" from the start.

CHAPTER EIGHTEEN

A Bucket of Fish

The next journey took me to the Philippine Islands. I had been in correspondence with Rev. C. R. Cortez, President of the Far East Bible Institute. Rev. Cortez had been led of God to start the Bible Institute in Tuguegarao. God had so mightily blessed his work that he now had a fellowship of over 100 churches and pastors, as well as a thriving Bible school. It was upon his invitation that I decided to make this next journey. It was good to know that this time Ruth could come along.

I had learned that nothing is ever done for God without problems; problems are the price of progress. Ruth and I felt sure that if we were to do anything constructive in the Philippines, God would allow our faith to be tested by many problems.

When we landed in Manila, we were to change planes and fly on to the city of Tuguegarao on a Philippine Airlines' plane. I was scheduled to begin a seminar at the Far East Bible Institute the next day; it was important for us to make good connections. But when we tried to get tickets, the agent said, "I'm sorry; there is no space available."

"Then perhaps there is another airline?" I suggested.

"No, sir," he replied. "The Philippine Airlines is the only one making flights into Tuguegarao."

"Well, then, perhaps we can take the next flight."

"I'm sorry, sir, but all available space is sold out on each daily flight for the next two weeks." (Planes are the only good method of transportation in the Philippines and many people travel this way.)

I turned to Ruth. "What are we going to do?" I said helplessly. "We're stuck!"

She tried to swallow her smile, but a little bit of it slid across her face anyway. "We could try praying," she said.

That's what we did. Finding a not-so-private corner, we bowed our heads and prayed, "Lord, get us out of this mess."

We knew there was no point in taking a bus. Bus travel is almost impossible in that area. So a kind friend drove us to the nearest travel agency 3 or 4 miles away. There we put in another appeal for space on the very same flight we'd asked the ticket agent about. But again we were told, "There is absolutely no space."

Still believing God for a miracle, we went on back to the airport and tried again to get tickets.

"No, sir," the agent said. "All seats are taken."

So we stood there wondering what to do. In five more minutes, the plane would take off for Tuguegarao.

"Father," I prayed, "You've *got* to do something. We're on Your business, and if You want us to get to Tuguegarao, You'll have to make a way."

I had no sooner prayed that prayer than the ticket agent called our names and told us there were two unclaimed seats. Grabbing our bags, we ran for the plane.

"Thank You, Jesus! Thank You Jesus!" I was saying with every step.

We received a warm welcome at the Far East Bible Institute. Brother Cortez had done everything possible to prepare for our coming, and I felt in my spirit that these were going to be spiritually profitable days for all of us.

239

We soon found out that the Holy Spirit had already been working here, as in almost every part of the world. There was a great interest in the power of the Holy Spirit, and in every seminar there were around 150 ministers present from various denominations, along with the students and many other people. Denominational differences didn't seem to enter their minds. The Holy Spirit had brought them together in the fellowship of Jesus, and they rejoiced in Him as they packed the auditorium for every service.

Among the powerful manifestations of the Holy Spirit throughout the services, one stands out. A young lady by the name of Betty Reyes had been attending our services. Betty was a very fine Christian girl, and a student at the Methodist College in Cabanatuan. That night, she stood up rather unexpectedly near the beginning of the service and began moving from person to person, laying her hands on them and prophesying under the anointing of the Holy Spirit. To one after another, she spoke of their personal needs— needs which only the Holy Spirit could have revealed to her. To others, she spoke of the ministry and spiritual gifts which the Holy Spirit was imparting to them. Sensing that this particular manifestation was quite new to the people, I observed Betty very carefully. I was greatly concerned that everything be done in the Spirit and in harmony with the

Word of God. But the longer I watched her, the more relaxed I became. There was no question in my mind that she was prophesying in the Spirit, just as the daughters of Philip had done in Bible times. I will never forget the remarkable way the Holy Spirit used Betty to minister to the needs of the people that night. But I could see that Brother Cortez was uneasy.

"Brother Rasmussen," he whispered, "don't you think it's time for you to take over?" He was quite concerned that something might get out of control. And Ruth told me later that his wife, Hosana, was just as nervous as her husband.

"Brother Cortez," I said kindly, "there's nothing to fear. Everything is under the control of the Holy Spirit, and we must let Him do His work."

And how glad I was that I did not interfere! Through the ministry of that young girl, the Lord's presence became so manifest that many fell under the power of God. This resulted in many turning to God. When I gave the invitation, it seemed that almost everyone came forward. Oh, what praying there was that night! Many were saved, and many others received the baptism in the Spirit.

The meetings continued with great anointing and power. One day Brother Cortez said to me, "Brother Rasmussen, we've never experienced anything like this—the teaching, the revelation from the Word, the impact of the Holy Spirit. It's all so marvelous!"

"It's the Lord's doing," I replied.

"Yes," he said, "isn't Jesus wonderful? Do you know, before these meetings, we were having quite a problem with our national pastors getting discouraged and resigning. But now there is such a renewing and reviving that they're coming to me and saying, 'Brother Cortez, we're not going to give up; we're going back to our churches.' "

"Praise the Lord!" I said happily. I knew this outpouring of the Holy Spirit would continue to bear fruit for many years to come.

While we were there, the Lord gave us a great opportunity to preach the Gospel over station DZCV in Tuguegarao. We had two half-hour broadcasts daily for the duration of our stay in the Philippines, and were able to reach about seven million people every day. God used these broadcasts, and we received reports of some who were saved and healed through that ministry. Others came to our meetings at the Bible Institute because of what they had heard on the air.

In addition to the seminars and the radio broadcasts, we were able to make quite a number of trips out to various villages to preach Jesus. We found many, many lovely

Roman Catholic people in these villages; but like the Protestants, many of them were Christians in name only, and did not really know Jesus. So I would preach my simple message to them, and it was common to see many of them accepting Jesus as their personal Savior. It thrilled me to see the Holy Spirit working so mightily among these dear people. It seemed that God was pouring out His Spirit everywhere! But the greatest thrill was yet to come.

I had asked Brother Cortez if he would direct me to some tribespeople who had never yet heard the Gospel. God had laid on my heart the importance of finding the unreached in every country where I traveled. My first priority was to take the Gospel to these people, no matter how long it took to get there, and no matter what means of conveyance I had to use. I was very happy the day Brother Cortez told me he had arranged a trip for us.

"Where are we going?" I asked him, eager to push out to new frontiers.

"Why, we're going out to visit a tribe of headhunters."

"Headhunters!" I gulped in disbelief. "You mean *real* headhunters?"

"Yes—what's the matter, don't you want to go?"

"Well, er—ah—yes, I guess so. I just didn't expect . . . ." I could just see my dried head hanging in some native's collection, swinging in the breeze!

Then I told Ruth.

"Headhunters!" she exclaimed. "You mean *real* headhunters?" It sounded like an instant re-play. She began to speak about 140 words a minute, with gusts up to 195. But Brother Cortez assured us there would be no problems.

"These people don't hunt heads anymore," he explained. Then, with a twinkle in his eye, he added, "Of course, if they found an especially nice one like yours, Ruth, you never know *what* they might do!" We laughed hilariously, but Ruth was not amused.

The next morning, Brother Cortez, his wife Hosana and daughter Leoning, plus Ruth and I and eleven other Filipino Christians crowded into a jeep land rover and started the journey down to a coastal town. Messengers were sent ahead of us, to inform the headhunters that we were coming.

By the time we reached the coastal town from which we were to go by boat to the headhunters' island, a storm seemed to be brewing and the sea was already quite choppy. Some of our party questioned the advisability of getting out on the ocean; but since the headhunters were expecting us, we decided to take the chance.

On the coast, 21 more Filipinos joined us, making 37 of us all told. Brother Cortez had arranged for us to make the short voyage in two outrigger boats. The first boat had an outboard motor on it, and the second boat was tied on some distance behind. As we were waiting to get started, I looked out over the grayish-green sea and breathed a silent prayer, while the incoming waves slipped-slapped against the sides of our boats.

In a few minutes, we were out to sea. The waves were now breaking, and the whitecaps were rolling in. Our two boats heaved and rolled along. I realized they weren't very seaworthy, but we were trusting God to give us traveling mercies.

After traveling for quite some time, we came to a place where we could beach our boats and refuel. Everybody got out of the boats to stretch, while we were refueling.

A short time later, we all got back into the boats and headed for the open seas. On the way out, we found ourselves in dangerous waters where there were many coral reefs. The breakers were dashing over them and splashing foam high into the air. I knew the danger. If one of our boats should get caught on a reef, those large breakers could easily capsize it.

"Lord," I said, "You see the danger we're in —but we're on a mission for You. Please keep us from all harm."

Suddenly our boat gave a terrible lurch, and I heard the motor sputtering and laboring, on the verge of stalling. Instinctively, I looked back at the boat in tow. It had struck a reef!

We revved up our motor and tried to pull ahead, but the boat wouldn't budge; it was lodged solidly. Some of the men on that boat got poles and tried to push it off, but it was hopeless. The breakers were dashing against that poor little boat; it groaned and shuddered under the force of those mighty waters. I knew no one in that boat could swim. If the boat capsized, it would be a terrible tragedy.

"If we all drown out here," I thought to myself, "what a victory that would be for the devil! He doesn't want us to go out to those headhunters, and so if he can drown us, that's exactly what he will do." But I felt sure that God had a way out for us.

Leaning over toward my wife, I said, "Ruth, we must agree together in prayer!" We joined hands, and there on that rough, windy sea, we prayed.

"Father, in the name of Jesus," I prayed desperately, "send a swell to lift that boat off the reef, and set us free!"

I had no sooner uttered that prayer than a great swell rolled in and lifted that boat with a mighty upsurge, and suddenly we were free again. You can be sure there was a lot of praising going on in that boat as we finished our journey!

We landed on the shore of a little island late that day. As we got out of our boats, the tribespeople came out of the forests where they had been waiting. I tried not to remember that they were headhunters.

We found out through an interpreter that many of the other tribes had gathered and waited for us throughout the day. But when they saw the storm coming, they said, "They'll never make it." Hours before we arrived, they had dispersed and gone back into the forest. However, this one tribe lived right there on the coast, and so we still had a congregation even though we were very late.

First of all, we presented them with some gifts, as is customary when you meet a tribal chief and his people. There were many "Oooos" and "Ahhhhs" as they admired the things we had brought them, and chief Ungar seemed very grateful.

Then we were led to a large hut, and I assumed this was where we would have our meeting. I noticed there were no idols in sight, and I wondered what sort of religion these people had, and what they worshiped.

"Chief Ungar," I asked through my interpreter once we were inside the hut, "do you believe there is a God?"

"Yes," he answered thoughtfully. "I believe there is a God. Somebody made these trees," he said, pointing through the open windows to

247

palms and other luxurious foliage around the hut. "And Somebody made the sea," he continued, stretching his hands out toward the ocean. Then, pointing his finger toward the sky, he said, "Somebody put the stars up there, and Somebody put the sun and moon there. But," he said, "I don't know Him."

Well! That was all he needed to say! "Chief," I said, "Him whom you believe in and do not know, I have come to declare to you." And I began in a very simple way to tell him about Jesus. "Jesus is the God who made all these things," I said. " 'All things were made by him, and without him was not anything made that was made.' He is the 'Light which lighteth every man that cometh into the world.' He was with the Father from the beginning. It is Jesus who created the trees, the ocean, the stars, the moon, the sun and everything else you see."

Then I went on and told him the simple story of how Jesus came down to earth to shed His blood as a sacrifice for sin and atone for the sins of the world.

"Chief," I continued, "Jesus died for you and your people, as well as for all people. Jesus *loves you!* He has not forgotten you. That's why He has sent us."

The story touched his heart. It was beautiful to watch the Holy Spirit giving understanding to those primitive tribespeople. You

could almost see their faces light up with understanding.

"Chief Ungar," I said, "would you like to
accept Jesus as your God? Would you like to
have Him as your Savior? Would you accept
His shed blood as an atonement for all your
sins, and become a child of God this very
day?"

"Oh, yes!" He said.

Then I turned to the rest of the tribe and
asked them the same question. They watched
their chief to see if it was all right, and he began to beckon them to come. They had
been taught that whatever the chief does and
recommends to the people is right to do. So
the whole tribe gave their hearts to Jesus, and
the Spirit was poured out upon them.

There were many who were sick. As we laid
our hands on them and prayed, God healed
them instantly by His power. Their faith was
greatly strengthened when they saw the power
of Jesus being manifested right before their
very eyes.

I don't think I ever saw a more grateful
man than Chief Ungar. His face was literally
aglow. Pointing to me, he said to his interpreter, "Does this man eat fish?"

"Yes," I told the interpreter, "I love it!"

And then I saw clearly what he was about
to do. He wanted to thank me in some way.
They had no money, so he couldn't give an
offering as American Christians do. But his

heart had been deeply touched, and he wanted to do something for me.

So while we continued to enjoy sweet fellowship, he sent his son out to sea. In a short time, he came back with a bucketful of beautiful sea fish. And the chief brought them to me as his love offering. I want you to know that bucket of fish meant more to me than a brick of gold. It came from a heart full of love. It came from a heathen man who had heard about Jesus for the first time, and accepted Him and recommended Him to his tribe.

It was late in the evening when we left that island. It was hard to leave them. There was a lump in my throat as we got back into our boats and headed home. Dusk was creeping across the sky. By the time we finally pulled up to shore, the stars were twinkling overhead. I put my bucket of fish in the jeep, and we started our drive back to Tuguegarao.

"Brother Cortez," I said, "we've got to do something for those people. They need teaching so they can grow. It isn't right to bring lambs to life and then let them die in the wilderness."

"You're right," he said. "The lambs must be fed."

We drove on in silence. All I could think about was the thousands upon thousands of people I had seen all over the world who needed someone to love and teach them . . . .

Before we left the Philippines, we had an opportunity to journey up into the mountainous jungle areas of Luzon to visit the aborigenes. We were told that these people had never seen a white man before, so we knew it would be an interesting experience.

We left Tuguegarao around 3 or 4 in the morning, again taking along quite a number of Filipino Christians. It would be a long journey, and we wanted sufficient time to minister to these people once we got there. Soon the hot sun was up, and it was a beautiful golden day. The land rover jiggled along the narrow road for about six hours. We talked and had wonderful fellowship together for miles and miles.

Finally, we came to the Cagayan River. There was no bridge, but some enterprising citizens had invented a crude ferry which regularly carried passengers and vehicles across the river.

Brother Cortez told the owner of the ferry what we wanted, and then I got out and watched with interest as they prepared to take our jeep across. The ferry was made of two large canoes. These canoes were huge, hollowed-out trees that would hold perhaps 55 or 60 people each. They had been carefully placed side by side, but about ten feet apart. Then planks had been placed across these canoes.

251

"Do they intend to take our jeep across on *that* contraption?" I asked myself.

After looking it over more carefully though, I saw that it was really quite sturdy, and I became more confident that we would have no trouble getting across. The ferry even had a canvas roof over part of the deck to shield the passengers from the hot sun. We were going to be traveling first-class!

The laborers proceeded to lay planks to form a ramp from the shore to the ferry, and the jeep was driven up onto it. Then they motioned for the passengers to get on board, and an outboard motor on the back of one of the canoes was started. In a short time, we were across.

Finally we were on our way again, and drove for a couple more hours into the jungle. It was somewhere around noon when we arrived at the crude village of those aborigenes people.

We must have seemed as strange to them as they did to us. Ruth and I were the first white people they had ever seen, and they drew back from us when we tried to approach them. They were all completely naked, except for a little loincloth. The poverty, ignorance and superstition were apparent everywhere we looked. We learned later that they sustain life by hunting wild pigs and deer with bows and arrows and spears, and by picking wild fruits and berries. It was hard for me to believe that this was in the 1970's!

At first, we thought they were afraid of us, but the interpreter told us later that they thought we were gods. You can hardly imagine how helpless we felt as we stood there before those people, wondering what we could do for them in such a short time!

But then a Voice within me said, "*All they need is love.*"

Ruth must have gotten the same guidance, because she was soon standing in front of a little mother who was holding a naked baby, trying to love them both.

"What is the baby's name?" she asked through the interpreter.

"She has no name," the mother replied.

"No name?" Ruth was surprised, because the child was obviously almost 6 months old. "Andrew," she said, calling to me, "look, this child has no name. Can't *we* give her a name?"

"Okay," I said, "how about calling her Ruth?"

We learned later why the child had no name. We were told that the aborigenes do not give names to their children until they are at least a year old, because so many of them die in infancy.

So we asked the mother if we could name the child Ruth; she was delighted. Ruth tenderly picked up the little child and cuddled her as though she were her own. Together, we laid our hands on little Ruthie and dedicated her and her parents to the Lord Jesus.

In a short time we called the people together, and through an interpreter I told them the story of Jesus as simply as I could. Again, I saw the same manifestation of the Spirit that I had seen in so many places, as Jesus was revealed to them and they were given an understanding of their need for Him. It was beautiful to see how they responded. When I gave the invitation, I could hardly believe my eyes. Almost every one of them accepted Jesus as his Savior!

As we drove home that night, I marveled at how eagerly they had received our message—just as people had almost everywhere we had gone. Surely, this was the doing of the Holy Spirit. A new spiritual phenomenon was taking place all over the world. We had been receiving reports of this spiritual outpouring from many of our own missionaires, as well as others. Now we had seen a little bit of it for ourselves.

"Ruth," I said after much thought, "this is the last big sweep. All over the world, the harvest is dead ripe."

"I know," she said, "I wonder how much time we have left to gather it in."

CHAPTER NINETEEN

Prophecies Unfolding

Ruth and I were shocked to find so many changes when we returned to the Philippine Islands in 1972. Communist infiltrators had been busy during the year, and there was a certain fearfulness in the air. Much of the old freedom we had enjoyed the year before was gone. But in spite of all that, there was much rejoicing when we returned to Tuguegarao. Hosana, Brother Cortez's wife, met us at the airport, and embraced up both with tears. She then explained that her husband was in Manila trying to get a truck released which had been donated by a church in the States.

After chattering for a few minutes, we picked up our bags and hailed a taxi—a two-wheeled cart pulled by a little Filippino horse, no bigger than a Shetland pony. We had a great deal of luggage, so we piled that in first. Then Hosana and Ruth climbed up into the cart, and I looked at that little horse.

"You'd better be more than a one-horse-power horse," I thought as I climbed up into the cart—all 200 pounds of me. The driver said something in his native tongue and slapped the reins, and the little horse tried to move. But there was so much weight on the back of the cart that it was almost lifting the little fellow off his feet, and he just couldn't get any traction. I thought it was a little bit funny, but the driver made some angry remarks and jumped off the cart. In a few minutes he had our luggage moved up ahead of the axle; then he got back on the cart, very close to the horse, and we started off.

When we arrived at the Far East Bible Institute we were greeted by a great crowd of students and pastors who were singing a welcome song for us. When we stepped off the cart, they came and put lei after lei around our necks, and embraced us over and over. Unbidden tears came to our eyes as we realized how much they loved us.

But we soon noticed certain differences. Many of the people were greatly concerned about the war in Viet Nam. It appeared that the President of the United States was being pressured into bringing a swift end to this long, drawn-out war. People all over the Orient were fearful that if Saigon fell to the

Communists, that part of the world would no longer be free. The Communists were working hard to bring pressure on many of the free governments in that part of the world. And this was true in the Philippines.

Since the seminars had been such a success the year before, Brother Cortez thought we ought to attempt something bigger this year, so he had secured the 20,000-seat arena in the city of Ilagan. The crusade had been highly advertised in the newspaper long before we arrived. I was looking forward to a mighty outpouring of the Holy Spirit in that arena.

However, shortly before we arrived, there had been trouble. During a festival in a nearby town, some Communists had thrown bombs into a crowd, and quite a number had been killed or wounded.

Not long after that, a representative of the Philippine army came to the Bible Institute. "Mr. Cortez," he said, "we recommend that you do not carry on with this crusade at this time. The Communists will seek to terrify you, and they will undoubtedly use bombs. There will be killings and wounded people, and nothing but misery will result."

Cortez thought it over, and prayed about it. Finally he decided that it would be for the good of everybody to postpone the meeting and instead carry on with our seminars as we had the previous year.

However, even the seminars were different. Though the joy of the Lord was greatly manifest, still there was a certain heaviness in the air which I had not sensed before. But it was not inexplainable. I knew there were pastors in those meetings who had come from a distance, and whose families were in danger. We sensed this nervousness especially in the night services, for this was when the Communists usually struck. We all knew that there was the possibility of danger—even death. Many of the pastors stayed only a few days, and then went back home. "Our families are in danger," they said. "We must be with them."

One pastor came down from Isabela Province at great risk. He not only wanted to attend our meetings, but he also wanted to see his brother, who had been attending the services.

"I am one of four marked men," he told us soberly. "Three have already been liquidated, and I am next. I don't know when my life may be snuffed out."

Before he left, he told his brother how he wanted his affairs settled after he was gone. After a few days, he went back to his family. "I am not afraid," he said. "I am willing to lay down my life for Jesus." He went away with great joy, knowing full well that death might be near.

Although the meetings were different from

those we'd had the year before, I was glad to be there. I knew they needed my ministry now more than ever, and we received much blessing through one another's fellowship.

One night about midnight, there was rapid rifle fire not more than a quarter of a mile from the Bible Institute grounds. Ruth awoke with a start.

"Andrew!" she called. "Andrew! Isn't that rifle fire?" She had been in Germany during World War II, and the sound was very familiar. The city in which she lived had been completely demolished by bombs and artillery. She knew the horrors of war. The rapid cracking of a rifle excited old fears very deep within her. I propped myself up on one elbow and listened. "Yes," I said, "that *is* rifle fire."

She began to cry.

"Don't be afraid," I said, trying to comfort her. "It's all right."

"Why did we have to come out here and endanger our lives?" she blurted out, weeping.

"Ruth," I said, "*Jesus* is here with us. If we have to go this way, well—what a fine way to lay down our lives for Him."

"Well, what are we going to do?" she asked.

"Let's just hold steady," I suggested. "We need to set an example for these people."

I got up and dressed and spent the rest of

the night in prayer, asking for God's protection. The rifle fire died down, and the next morning everything seemed back to normal.

It was Sunday morning. The students gathered in the chapel for the worship service; it promised to be an unusual meeting. God swept over those students in a great spirit of prayer. By the time I was to preach, I knew I had to teach them about the coming of Jesus.

"He may come at any time," I said, "and we need to be ready. But if we must lay down our lives for Him before He comes, then let's be ready to do that too."

I went on to encourage them. "The Communists are trying to cause trouble in many parts of the world, but I want you to know that God is greater than the Communists, and He is pouring out His Spirit all over the world. The Church is becoming stronger and stronger. So 'lift up your heads'," I exhorted. " 'Your redemption draweth nigh!' Let's not be slack in the work the Lord has given to us. This Gospel must be preached in every nation, every kindred and every tribe. And then the Lord shall come!"

So they were greatly encouraged to continue in the work God had given them, even in the midst of their trouble. I was convinced that God would use this testing-time to strengthen them in their faith.

While we were there, we had the opportunity of going back up to visit the same aborigines tribe we had visited on our previous trip. Both Ruth and I were eager to see how our "Gospel seed" had grown. Furthermore, it would be a welcome change to be away from the pressure-cooker situation in Tuguegarao.

When we finally arrived at the little jungle village, we could hardly believe what we saw. The natives rushed out to greet us, taking our hands in theirs and squeezing them tightly. Then they bowed and placed their foreheads on the backs of our hands, showing that we were accepted and welcomed. What a contrast to the cautious way we had been received a year before! Another striking thing was that many of them were now wearing clothes. The students from the Bible Institute had gone up there after our first visit, and had taken clothing to them. Some of the clothes were quite worn out—more like rags than clothes. But they used what they had to cover their bodies as best they could.

Then we saw that little mother coming, with baby Ruth toddling along at her side. She took that child and presented her to Ruth; and, oh, what a sweet reunion there was! Ruth took the little child into her arms and hugged her close.

"I've got something for you!" she said. Opening a bag, she brought out a little skirt and blouse which she had bought for baby

Ruth in Toguegarao. After she had put them on her, the mother danced up and down in delight.

But the greatest joy of all was to find the natives continuing to follow Jesus. Through the ministry of several national workers three churches had been started, and building materials were being trucked in so that they could have a place of worship. Plans were also being made to send in a competent teacher to show them how to read the Bible.

I knew we owed so much to the national workers. They were responsible for the continuation of what we had started, and it was wonderful to be associated with such dedicated servants of the Lord. We had also heard glowing reports of progress from Chief Ungar and his island-tribe; this too was due to the follow-up and teaching ministry of the national workers.

"What a pity!" I thought as I stood there watching those simple aborigenes people. "They have been neglected for so long. They are left alone back here in the wilderness, and few people care." That day we baptized twelve more converts before we left.

As we traveled towards Tuguegarao that night, I rejoiced that another tribe had heard the message of the Gospel. That meant we were that much closer to the day of Jesus' return.

On the way back to the States, I found myself thinking more and more about the coming
of Jesus. I knew it couldn't be far off. I
thought back over a number of significant
events which had taken place within the previous twenty-five years or so of my life—
events that seemed to prove beyond any
doubt that we were living in the closing hours
of this age . . . .

My mind went back to the month of May,
1948, when I had attended that convention
in Saskatchewan, Canada, where the prophecy
had been given about the outpouring of the
Holy Spirit upon people of all denominations.
It was during that convention that I walked
into the lobby of the hotel where I was
staying and noticed the daily newspaper. The
headlines were printed in big, black letters,
about two inches high:

ISRAEL IS A NATION FOR THE
FIRST TIME IN 2,000 YEARS

I had to buy that paper. I got on the elevator and began to read while we were going up.
As my eyes raced down through the article, I
could hardly believe what I was reading. The
Jewish National Council and the General
Zionist Council had met at Tel Aviv to pro-
claim the establishment of a Jewish State to
be called *Israel*. David Ben Gurion had been
appointed Prime Minister.

I knew that this was of great prophetic significance. For over 2,000 years the Jews had been a homeless people, wandering over the face of the earth, finding citizenship wherever they could. God had said it would be that way. But I also knew that the greatest sign of the near return of Jesus would be the restoration of the Jews, and their recognition as a nation. And here it was, right in front of my eyes!

It's a good thing I didn't do what I felt like doing in that elevator. I was so overjoyed I could hardly contain myself. I felt like giving everybody a big hug and shouting, "Praise the Lord! He's coming back!" But I decided I'd better act a little more dignified until I could get to my room.

When I closed that door behind me, I threw up my hands and began to rejoice.

"Thank You, Jesus! Thank You, Jesus!" I said. "You have worked a wonder. Surely, now, Your coming cannot be far away!"

Then I sat down at the table in that hotel room and laid my Bible and the newspaper side by side. Remembering the passage about the dry bones in Ezekiel 37, I turned to that chapter, and there in verse 11, I read these words:

Then he said unto me, Son of man, these bones are the whole house of Israel: behold, they say, Our bones are dried, and our hope is lost: we are cut off for our parts.

264

What an exact picture that was of the attitude of the Jewish people for the past 2,000 years! To them it seemed utterly impossible that they would ever again be a nation. Most of them had given up all hope of any such development. I think my heart pounded a little faster when I read the next three verses:

Therefore prophesy and say unto them, Thus saith the Lord God; Behold, O my people, I will open your graves, and cause you to come up out of your graves, and bring you into the land of Israel.

And ye shall know that I am the Lord, when I have opened your graves, O my people, and brought you up out of your graves,

And shall put my spirit in you, and ye shall live, and I shall place you in your own land: then shall ye know that I the Lord have spoken it, and performed it, saith the Lord.

So there it was in prophecy! And here it was in the newspaper! "Oh, thank You, Jesus!" I cried.

I knew the newspaper account was just the beginning though, for there were two things prophesied here about the Jewish people: their return to the land of Israel, and the outpouring of the Spirit upon them. No doubt, this returning and outpouring process would involve a number of years—but at least, we were in the beginnings!

I remembered a passage in Hosea 6 which had to do with the restoration of Israel, so I quickly turned to that place. Here, in verses 1 and 2, were the prophesied words of the nation of Israel during this restoration process:

Come, and let us return unto the Lord: for he hath torn, and he will heal us; he hath smitten, and he will bind us up.

After two days will he revive us: in the third day he will raise us up, and we shall live in his sight.

I was about to read on, but something drew my attention back to those words, "after *two days* will he revive us . . . ." I looked again at the newspaper headlines:

ISRAEL IS A NATION FOR THE FIRST TIME IN 2,000 YEARS

Two days. Two thousand years. Suddenly, I remembered II Peter 3:8:

But, beloved, be not ignorant of this one thing, that one day is with the Lord as a thousand years, and a thousand years as one day.

I saw the meaning in a flash. Israel's two prophetic days had been fulfilled in those 2,-000 years. Now they were being revived, and the third day was being ushered in. I looked again. Yes, that's what it said: ". . . *in the third day he will raise us up, and we shall live in his sight.*" And if I had any question about the relationship of the restoration of Israel to the second coming of Jesus, it was all clarified in verse 3:

Then shall we know, if we follow on to know the Lord: his going forth is prepared as the morning; and he shall come unto us as the rain, as the latter and former rain unto the earth.

It was so clear now. Israel must be restored, first nationally, then spiritually. *Then* the Lord will come. It came to me very forcibly as Ruth and I winged our way home from the Philippines that His coming could not be far off. I tingled with excitement at the mere thought of it.

My mind also went back to an experience I had in the late 1960's. Ruth and I had been traveling down the Pennsylvania Turnpike, on our way to White Plains, New York. Knowing I was tired, Ruth had taken the wheel to give me a short rest. As we drove along, I began to think about the Six-day War, and the circumstances which led up to it.

I recalled how trouble had been brewing between the Arabs and Israel for some time. Egypt had been mobilizing troops in the Sinai Peninsula. Nasser had requested that the United Nations withdraw their peace-keeping forces from the Gaza Strip. And to make matters worse, Nasser and Hussein had made an agreement, and Egyptian officers had taken command of the Jordanian army.

There was no question about it—Nasser was concentrating on a massive Arab build-up which he hoped would be able to wipe out Israel. He had even printed a commemorative stamp in remembrance of the destruction of Israel. It had been printed in advance, so certain was he of victory. I had a hobby of collecting stamps and was quite interested in this one. In the background was a map of Israel going up in flames; in the foreground was a superimposed picture of Nasser. It depicted in a vivid way his vow to destroy Israel.

Then, I remembered how, on June 5, 1967, the startling news came of war in the Middle East. Tiny Israel with her three million people was threatened with total destruction at the hands of eighty million angry Arabs, supported by Russia and her satellites.

But to the amazement of the whole world, the news came the next day that the old city of Jerusalem had been taken by the Israeli army. At that point, the battle raged on with a series of incredible victories for Israel, and in six short days it was all over, the Arabs having been whipped so badly that they were embarrassed in front of the whole world. Besides that, Israel had gained some valuable territory from the hands of the Arabs.

I was quietly meditating about the meaning of all this as we rolled down the turnpike. Neither of us had spoken for some time. *As I was staring out the windshield blankly, I saw a word hovering in front of me in gold letters: "EZEKIEL."*

"Ezekiel?" I thought to myself. "Ezekiel

268

what?" *And the figure "33" appeared. It hovered there for a brief moment, then vanished.*

I glanced at Ruth for a moment, wondering if I should tell her.

"Ruth," I said, "I've just seen a beautiful vision."

"Really?"

"Yes, I saw golden letters in front of my eyes, spelling out Ezekiel 33."

"Ezekiel 33. Isn't *that* strange?"

"What do you suppose it means?"

"Well," she said, "why don't you turn to it? There's my Bible."

I read the passage aloud. God was telling Ezekiel about his duties as a watchman of the house of Israel. He was to keep Israel informed of any significant events to come. Like a watchman on the city wall, he was to warn them about the dangers of sin and the sure judgment that would follow. Verses 7 and 8 seemed to stand out to me as I read:

So thou, O son of man, I have set thee a watchman unto the house of Israel; therefore thou shalt hear the word of my mouth, and warn them from me.

. . . if thou dost not speak to warn the wicked from his way, that wicked man shall die in his iniquity; but his blood will I require at thine hand.

After I had finished reading, I sat quietly for a while. "Ruth," I said after a moment, "do you realize what a tremendous responsi-

269

bility that places upon us? If we fail to warn people about the consequences of sin, then the guilt of *their* sins will be on *us*."

"It's absolutely frightening, isn't it?" she said.

"That's right," I said. "God holds us responsible for the sins of other people, and we're not released from that responsibility until we have warned them."

"And not only that," she added, "but their blood is going to be required at our hands."

"That's right," I answered. "And here is something else. Ezekiel was made a watchman for the *whole* house of Israel. He had to answer for the whole nation, not just for his relatives or his neighbors."

"What does that mean?" she asked.

"Well, Ruth, in New Testament terms, I think it means that the overseers of the Church are responsible to warn the Church and the nation of the dangers of sin. We are the night watchmen. When we see the Church becoming lukewarm, we are to cry out a warning. When we see our nation becoming immoral and rebellious, we are responsible to warn everyone we can. When we see Christians becoming worldly and forgetting the promise of Jesus' return, we are responsible to warn them."

"And if we don't?"

"If we don't, then God holds *us* responsible for their sins."

270

"Whew!"

"Remember what Jesus said about our being the salt of the earth? If the salt loses its savor, it's good for nothing—it might as well be thrown out. Ruth, the reason God has us here is to hold back the tide of sin, to warn people of the danger, to remind them that Jesus is coming back soon. If we don't do that, what good are we to God?"

"Yes, and what about the parable of the ten virgins?" Ruth said. "According to that parable, half of the people invited to the marriage aren't going to be ready when the Bridegroom comes."

"Yes, and do you know why? Because somebody failed to wake them up in time. Somebody failed to warn them."

"Andrew," she said, "He's coming soon, isn't He?"

"Everything points that way, dear."

"Then we've got a big job ahead of us, haven't we?"

"Very big," I replied. "Without the mantle, we'll never get it done."

"The mantle? *What* mantle?"

"The mantle of the Holy Spirit," I replied. "Without that, the task is hopeless."

What memories these were! As our jet flew high over the Pacific, heading homeward from the Philippines, I saw in a new way that the Church was undergoing a major transformation. A new day was dawning for the Church, just as it was dawning for Israel. Both of these events, I knew, were merely two great tributaries pouring into the great river of Biblical prophecy, swiftly moving on to the return of Jesus.

CHAPTER TWENTY

Maranatha!

When we arrived back in San Diego, I was flooded with reports of revival. Dusty old churches all over the country were coming alive once again. Neighborhood prayer groups were springing up everywhere. Almost every Christian magazine and periodical was carrying reports of revival springing up all over the world.

"This is the working of the Holy Spirit," I said. "He is getting the Bride ready for the Bridegroom. He knows Jesus wants His Bride to be prepared, so He is giving her gifts and graces so that she might be decked in the righteousness of Christ, a glorious Church without spot or wrinkle."

Remembering a passage in the fourth chapter of Ephesians, I opened my Bible and began to read at verse 11:

And he gave some, apostles; and some, prophets; and some, evangelists; and some, pastors and teachers;

For the perfecting of the saints, for the work of the ministry, for the edifying of the body of Christ:

Till we all come in the unity of the faith, and of the knowledge of the Son of God, unto a perfect man, unto the measure of the stature of the fulness of Christ.

I was well aware that the five ministry-gifts mentioned here had been relegated to an earlier age by some of my brethren, but I saw no scriptural basis for this. I re-read the passage. *What had Jesus done?* "He gave some apostles ... prophets ... evangelists ... pastors and teachers." *For what purpose?* "For the perfecting of the saints, for the work of the ministry, for the edifying of the body of Christ." *For what period of time?* "Till we all come in the unity of the faith ... unto a perfect man, unto the measure of the stature of the fulness of Christ."

It seemed quite obvious to me that the Church had not yet reached that point! And if not, then the ministry-gifts mentioned here were still needed. All of them! This is exactly what we had been seeing in all of our travels. *From the day God began to restore Israel, He began simultaneously to restore gifts to the*

274

Church. Time and again we had seen the Holy Spirit imparting ministry-gifts through the laying on of hands and prophecy, as well as in other ways. To what purpose? That the Church might become "a glorious Church," a Bride ready for the return of the Bridegroom.

I turned to I Corinthians 12. I knew that along with the five ministry-gifts, there must also be a restoration of the nine spiritual gifts mentioned in verses 8-10:

For to one is given by the Spirit the word of wisdom; to another the word of knowledge by the same Spirit;

To another faith by the same Spirit; to another the gifts of healing by the same Spirit;

To another the working of miracles; to another prophecy; to another discerning of spirits; to another divers kinds of tongues; to another the interpretation of tongues.

I knew by experience how important these gifts are for the edification of the Church. For guidance we need a word of wisdom and a word of knowledge. For impossible obstacles we need a gift of faith. For sickness among us we need a gift of healing. For unbelievers we need the power to work miracles. For the development of the Church we need a gift of prophecy. For protection we need a gift of discerning spirits. For deeper worship we need the gifts of tongues and interpretation.

Of course, there were many who had been denying the existence of such gifts in the

Church today. But now, the miracle of it all! Just when everybody was saying God was dead and the Church was on its way out, there had arisen all through the Church multitudes of people who had received an outpouring of the Holy Spirit, and were speaking in tongues and manifesting all sorts of gifts! The old, organized Church blinked its eyes and said, "Gifts aren't for today. Just ignore them and they will go away."

But they didn't go away. Many Christians became convinced that the Church was experiencing a genuine visitation of the Holy Spirit. And, if so, I knew there would be no stopping it. I remembered the prophecy given at the 1948 convention in Saskatchewan about the Holy Spirit's being poured out on all denominations, and upon the Catholics. It was all coming true.

I recalled a vision I had had many years ago when I was serving the church in Edmonton. I had decided to spend some time praying in the church, and was kneeling at a pew when it came before me.

I saw myself kneeling at a pew, as, in fact, I was. But in the vision, I became aware that there was another person kneeling beside me. Opening my eyes just a little, I noticed a little pool of tears on the pew in front of this other person, whoever it was.

"Who is this?" I wondered. "And why the tears?" I lifted my eyes and saw a Catholic nun kneeling beside me. She was dressed, not in black, but in white—pure white.

As she prayed, she laid her hand on my shoulder. I felt great compassion and love emanating from her. I began to realize that this Catholic sister had the love of Christ in her heart and wanted that love to flow together with my love for Christ, that we might be one in Him. At the height of that awareness of love, the vision vanished.

I thought a great deal about that vision. As I began to see what God was doing among the Catholics, I began to understand that God wanted me to love the Catholic Christians just as much as my other Christian brethren, because they belong to Him just as much as we do.

I will have to confess, though, that at first I had some misgivings about mingling too closely with Catholics—and even the Spirit-filled ones bothered me some. But in 1971, God taught me a great lesson.

We were having a convention in Chicago, and I had invited Sister Clare to speak to us about the charismatic renewal in the Catholic Church. When she came to speak for the first service, she said to me, "Brother Rasmussen, God has been very good to us Catholics. As of today, there are thousands upon thousands of Catholics baptized in the Holy Spirit and speaking in other tongues as they did on the day of Pentecost!"*

I gulped in disbelief. "How wonderful!" I said. "Praise the Lord!"

When the time came for her to minister to us in that first service, we all felt a wonderful love flowing from her heart to ours. She was one of us. She identified with us because she was born again as we were, and we were as she was.

But the problem came the day she was teaching on prayer. Not that we disagreed with *everything* she said. But when she began to relate how she prayed to Mary and used her rosary beads, that was just too much! Of course, she was teaching exactly as she had been taught, and she believed it was right. And she was very sweet about it.

But was I ever in hot water! I had invited her to the convention, and some of the brethren were talking rather unkindly about the matter, and saying, "I told you so!" And I understood how they felt. But I wondered if our attitude was right. So I decided to talk with the Sister.

"Sister Clare," I said, "I believe, just as you do, that Mary was a wonderful woman. The Bible says she was a virgin, and God chose her and overshadowed her by the Holy Spirit so that she conceived and gave birth to

*Time Magazine reports *well over* 100,000 Catholic Pentecostals. (April 9, 1973, p. 91)

278

Jesus. But, although she was a wonderful woman, nowhere in the Bible does it say that we should pray to her—and I'm sure you believe that we should do everything according to the Bible. The Bible tells us that we should pray to the Father, and that the only mediator we need is Jesus."

I was afraid she might be angry with me, but I looked into her eyes and saw that same sweet spirit of love which we had all felt during the service.

"Is that the way it is, Brother Rasmussen?" she asked in childlike simplicity. "Oh, I'm so glad you told me! I *do* want to know the right way to pray. And from now on I'm going to do it that way!"

I marveled at her. Only the Holy Spirit could have made her that teachable. I knew from that point on that we had much more to learn from her.

After the convention was over, she said to me, "Brother Rasmussen, I know you invited me here to teach, but really, I've done so little. What I realize now is that I came to be taught. I have learned so much during this convention!"

That was when it began to dawn on me that God was doing a wonderful thing. A miracle was taking place within the Church. The old denominationalism was beginning to die. The Holy Spirit was bringing the Lord's people into unity. I could easily visualize the day when people would no longer be saying, "I'm a Catholic," or, "I'm a Lutheran," or, "I'm an Episcopalian," or, "I'm a Presbyterian." I knew the day was coming when all such child's play would be forgotten. There was something else far more important.

The simplicity of that one great essential was impressed upon me afresh one day in Spokane, Washington. A teen-aged girl stopped me on the street. She was wearing a pair of jeans and had a big Bible under her arm. Taking me by the arm, she said, "Mister, do you know Jesus?"

"Yes," I said, smiling at her, "I *do* know Jesus!"

"But," she said, "do you really know what I mean? I mean, do you have Jesus in your heart?"

"Yes, young lady," I said joyfully, "I have Jesus in my heart!"

"Oh, hallelujah! Hallelujah!" she said. "Then *you* know Jesus just like *I* know Jesus!"

When I walked away from that young girl, I realized anew that this was the simple common denominator that would bring us all together: *Do you know Jesus?* What a question!

"The Holy Spirit is bringing us back to the simple things," I said to myself one day. "He doesn't want us to be quibbling about little nonessentials. In the end, the restoration of

280

both Israel and the Church will bring us all together in Christ. That's where we're headed. That's the miracle of the last days: Protestants, Catholics, Jews, Hippies and what have you—all filled with the Spirit, and one in Christ."

I recalled the word the early Christians used when they met together and when they parted. "Maranatha!" they said. "The Lord is coming soon!" I had heard Spirit-filled Christians all over the world saying that to one another more and more. It was as though the Holy Spirit had mysteriously impressed it upon the minds of all who belong to Jesus.

But still the exact time is unknown. The day of the Lord will come as a thief in the night. And I am a watchman in the night, warning you to be ready.

Epilogue

One night, about 2 years after I had become a born-again Christian, I had a tremendous visionary experience in the old farmhouse in Minnesota. It was so real, it seems but yesterday. Any time I want to see it, I can see it. Any time I want to feel it, I can feel it.

In my vision, it was morning, and I was just waking up. I rubbed my eyes sleepily, stretched and yawned a few times, and then bounced out of bed.

When I came into the living room, my brother Art was there, looking out the window. He was very excited about something.

"Andrew!" he said breathlessly. "Look at that! Look at that!"

When I looked, I saw the most spectacular

sunrise I had ever seen in my life. The sun was blazing brighter and bigger than I had ever seen it before. Not a cloud was in the sky. Just those golden rays of sunlight bathing the whole countryside in yellow warmth.

"Oh, Art!" I exclaimed. "What a beautiful sunrise! I've never seen anything like that—never!"

Pointing to the sun, he said, "What makes it look so big?"

"I can't imagine," I said. "It's so different . . . ."

Suddenly, I felt a strange sensation in my body. A strong power came over me, and I felt my feet beginning to leave the floor. There was no effort on my part whatsoever. The floor began to get farther away, and in a moment my head was up to the ceiling. When I came to the ceiling, it seemed as though there were nothing solid there at all. It was like a vapor or a cloud, and I went straight through it, with nothing to stop me. Up, up I went, right through the roof of the house! I kept on going . . . and going . . . .

I looked aside, and there was Art going along with me! And then I became aware of others. There was Dad! There was one of the deacons from the church! There was a tribal chief from some island! There was a Catholic nun! There was a young girl in jeans! We were all floating off to somewhere, being drawn by some invisible power. I could see by now that

283

the sky was filled with millions of people, going up, up, up . . . .

Suddenly I realized we were up to the height of the moon and the stars. I looked out over the breathtaking spacescape and said in rapture, "Oh, what a wonderful feeling! The Lord has come! We're going up to meet Him!" I began to be aware of strength and vigor in my body such as I had never known before. There was nothing to hold me back.

"Just think!" I said to myself. "No more tears! No more sickness! No more weariness!"

Then I began to hear the singing of heavenly songs in the distance. I had never heard anything on earth to compare to it. As I looked up ahead, there was Jesus coming to meet us, and we were rising to meet Him in the air. What a thrill! When I saw Jesus, I thought I would burst for joy.

"Oh, Jesus!" I cried. "You said You'd come back! And You did!" And then all the millions of us took up a song, and it sounded even sweeter than the song of the angels as we sang, "My Jesus, I love Thee . . . I know Thou art mine . . . ."

And then the vision vanished, and I drifted off into a deep sleep.

When I woke up the next morning, I couldn't believe I was still on earth. I actually pinched myself to see if I was still flesh and blood.

"Well, Lord," I said, a little disappointed, "at least I know now how the last chapter ends."

And I got up to face a new day.

THE NEW WINE IS BETTER

by Robert Thom $1.45

Before the miracle happened, Robert Thom was an alcoholic sailor on the verge of suicide. Afterwards, his life was one miracle after another . . .

PLEASE MAKE ME CRY

by Cookie Rodriguez $1.45

The first female dope addict to "kick the habit" in Dave Wilkerson's ministry, Cookie was so hard people said even death didn't want her. Told the way it really happened, this is the story of how Cookie found Someone she wanted even more than heroin.

THE PURPLE PIG AND OTHER MIRACLES

by Dick Eastman $1.45

Hidden away in a rambling, wood frame house on "O" Street in Sacramento, there's a special underground room where Bible-believing Christians pray twenty-four hours a day, seven days a week. Miracles? They happen all the time. And the prayer power is spreading . . .

THE RAPTURE BOOK

by Doug Chatham $1.25

Almost everybody seems agreed that old planet Earth is a time-bomb about to go off, but here's a different slant—a slant which is backed up by the age-old prophecies of the Bible. Exciting teaching about the next event on the prophetic calendar!

SCANDALOUS SAINT

by John Hagee $1.25

The dynamic true story of John and Josie Eils, who were led by the Holy Spirit from one hair-raising scrape into another, only to escape by the skin of their teeth and the grace of God.

SIMMER DOWN, SAINT

by Jody Woerner $1.25

Anxious? Uptight? Lost your cool? Simmer down—and let the author show you how you can add health, strength, peace, and joy to your Christian experience through the power of the Holy Spirit.